FLIP-FLOP
paper piecing

Revolutionary Single-Foundation Technique • 52 Full-Size Patterns

mary kay mouton

C&T PUBLISHING

Text copyright © 2009 by Mary Kay Mouton

Artwork copyright © 2009 by C&T Publishing, Inc.

Publisher: **Amy Marson**

Creative Director: **Gailen Runge**

Acquisitions Editor: **Jan Grigsby**

Editor: **Liz Aneloski**

Technical Editors: **Helen Frost and Georgie Gerl**

Copyeditor/Proofreader: **Wordfirm Inc.**

Cover Designer/Book Designer: **Kristen Yenche**

Production Coordinator: **Zinnia Heinzmann**

Illustrator: **Richard Sheppard**

Photography by **Luke Mulks** and **Diane Pedersen** of C&T Publishing unless otherwise noted

Published by C&T Publishing, Inc., P.O. Box 1456, Lafayette, CA 94549

Library of Congress Cataloging-in-Publication Data

Mouton, Mary Kay,

 Flip-flop paper piecing : revolutionary single-foundation technique guarantees accuracy / Mary Kay Mouton.

   p. cm.

 Summary: "A new method of paper foundation piecing that enables the quilter to paper piece, on one foundation, what previously required multiple foundations. Instructions and full-size foundations (in 2 sizes) for 26 blocks. Project instructions for a sampler quilt that also includes appliqué. Also includes a small gallery"--Provided by publisher.

 ISBN 978-1-57120-540-7 (paper trade : alk. paper)

 1. Patchwork--Patterns. 2. Machine quilting--Patterns. I. Title.

 TT835.M75 2009

 746.46'041--dc22

                          2008023544

 Printed in China

 10 9 8 7 6 5 4 3 2 1

Dedication

To my daughter, Angie, who taught me everything I know about quilting.

Acknowledgments

Many thanks to my bee group, the Old Capital Stitchers—Kathy Boylan, Laurie Calvert, Gail Ellington, Betty Ivey, and Frances Rewis—and to our adopted member, Elizabeth Scott. These brave souls volunteered to be the first to try out my new piecing system and generously contributed their time and effort. Also, my gratitude to the staff at C&T, who kindly welcomed an outsider into their fold.

Contents

Introduction

Once upon a time, I was a pathetic patchwork piecer. My finished blocks were never the size they were supposed to be. My seams did not match. My points were neither crisp nor sharp. And you couldn't even talk to me about pieced borders. It made me very cranky.

I diligently tried and dismissed every piecing method known to humankind, until I discovered paper foundation piecing. This technique produced an accurate block with sharp points and straight lines. It was nearly perfect. Its only flaw was its limited range of block possibilities, but that was indeed a serious drawback. How many Log Cabin, Pineapple, or New York Beauty blocks do you want to make in a lifetime? It is possible to enlarge the range by subdividing blocks into two or three, or even eight or nine, foundation-pieced sections and then sewing those subdivisions together, but doesn't that defeat the purpose of sewing onto a paper foundation in the first place? Once again, you will have all those seams, all those opportunities for mismatched parts and random block sizing.

What I desperately needed was a new method of foundation piecing, one that could give me a wide variety of blocks, while using only one foundation as the base for each block. From that desperation came Flip-Flop Paper Piecing, a method of foundation piecing that enabled me to sew hundreds, even thousands, of blocks, each on its own single paper foundation.

The key to Flip-Flop Paper Piecing is the use of both sides of every foundation—the *Printed Side* of the foundation, on which the block is drawn, and the unprinted *Fabric Side* on which the fabric is placed. This book begins by explaining the construction of a block that illustrates that basic concept. Each chapter thereafter contains a new block that exemplifies an additional facet of Flip-Flop Paper Piecing. The lesson from each block applies specifically to that particular block but is also a principle of general use in Flip-Flop Paper Piecing. By the end of the book, all the basic techniques needed to flip-flop piece any flip-floppable block will have been presented.

GET STARTED

Paper-Piecing Basics

Flip-Flop Paper Piecing uses traditional paper-piecing methods but with the addition of some new techniques. Most quilters have tried traditional paper piecing. However, if you have not or if you'd like a quick refresher, read on. If you are a master paper piecer, feel free to skip the "Traditional Foundation Piecing" section of this chapter (page 9).

CHOOSING PAPER FOR FOUNDATIONS

In paper piecing, you have many choices of papers. Ideally, the paper should be crisp, thin, and easily torn but with enough strength to hold its shape firmly as you sew. I have yet to find that perfect paper.

The following are examples of different types of paper, with varying degrees of perfection:

- Regular photocopy or computer paper: I use this paper most often, because it is inexpensive, readily available, and holds together with heavy handling. It isn't a bad choice, but it is not crisp and stiff enough to be the paper of my dreams.

- Lightweight specialty papers produced specifically for foundation piecing: These papers are quite flimsy because they are designed for ease of paper removal. I find them to be too lightweight to hold their shapes firmly as I sew.

- Freezer paper: The advantage of freezer paper is that fabric will stick to the paper as you press each sewn piece into place. On the downside, freezer paper is more difficult to remove and is not firm enough to be my ideal choice.

- Scherenschnitte paper: Don't laugh, but this is my current favorite. It is nicely firm and holds its shape well, yet it is crispy and tears off easily.

- Water-soluble paper made specifically for foundation piecing: This paper is expensive. However, if you use it for miniatures, you don't need very much. It is, of course, the best choice in terms of ease of paper removal.

CREATING PAPER FOUNDATIONS

Any of the following methods can be used to make paper foundations:

- On graph paper, draw the necessary number of blocks to complete your quilt.

- Draw a single block on graph paper. Then copy it onto another piece of paper by tracing it over a lightbox or by machine sewing along the drawn lines with an unthreaded needle. (The needle will sew through the original onto another piece of paper placed under, and stapled to, the original.)

- Photocopy the number of blocks needed.

- Use a computer to scan or draw and then print the necessary number of blocks.

CUTTING FABRIC PIECES FOR PAPER PIECING

For best results, prewash all fabrics. This helps fusible web adhere to fabric.

One option is to create fabric pieces from small, leftover scraps or from chunks cut haphazardly. The only restriction is that the fabric pieces must be large enough to cover their numbered spaces plus the seam allowances around those spaces. I never choose this odd-chunk option, however, because I do not like the random grain lines produced. I also find it harder to sew with chunks that do not match the shapes of their numbered spaces.

Another option is to "precision" cut the fabric. Actually the cutting does not have to be all that precise. Each piece can be cut to match the general shape of the numbered space it will cover. Use scissors to cut around a template, or cut long strips with a rotary cutter and then subcut into shapes.

If you prefer to use cutting templates, as I do, trace the different pieces for each block onto graph paper. Use a ruler to add a ½" seam allowance along all sides. Because many pieces in a single block may be the exact same shape, such as a 2" square or a 2" half-square triangle, often a single cutting template can be used repeatedly in the construction of a block. The same cutting template can even be used for several blocks.

One word of warning when using cutting templates: Because foundation piecing involves placing fabric on the reverse side of a paper foundation, it is safest to place all templates on the wrong side of the fabric for cutting. If you make wrong-side cutting a habit, any pieces that have asymmetrical shapes will always be cut correctly.

A compromise between cutting random chunks and precision cutting is strip-piece cutting. With a rotary cutter, cut long strips that are wide enough to cover their allotted spaces. Subcut these strips into pieces as needed. I use this technique frequently, especially for squares and rectangles.

Whichever option you choose, be generous with the size. It is far easier to have extra fabric than to find that once a piece is sewn and flipped, it does not completely cover its numbered space.

TRADITIONAL FOUNDATION PIECING

Traditional foundation piecing is a flip-and-sew style of construction in which pieces of fabric are sewn onto paper foundations. Follow these steps to complete a Log Cabin block using traditional foundation piecing:

1. Copy the Log Cabin block pattern on this page onto a piece of paper. Enlarge it if you wish.

2. On the Printed Side of the paper foundation, number the pieces in sequential piecing order (that is, the order in which the pieces will be added to the block).

NOTE: Seams are sewn on the Printed Side of the foundation. Fabrics are placed on the unprinted Fabric Side of the foundation. The lines and numbers may be somewhat visible from the unprinted side, but they will be faint and will appear backward. For the Log Cabin, each side will look like this:

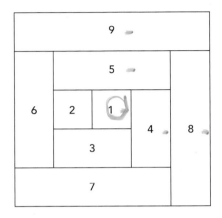

PRINTED SIDE

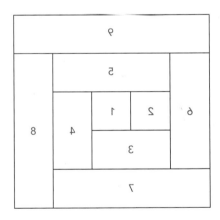

FABRIC SIDE
Numbers appear backward.

3. Cut the fabric for each numbered piece (page 8).

4. Beginning with piece 1, place the first piece of fabric right side up on the unprinted Fabric Side of the foundation. Be sure the area for piece 1 is covered and that there is an adequate (¼" or larger) seam allowance on all sides.

5. Place the second piece of fabric right side down on top of the first piece. Align piece 2 with piece 1, with raw edges overlapping the seamline between pieces 1 and 2. Be sure that once piece 2 is sewn and flipped, it will cover the entire area labeled "2" with an adequate seam allowance on all sides.

Pin or just hold the pieces in place. Note: I always pin. This allows me to do a test run by flipping piece 2 to be sure it covers its numbered space. I remove the pins as I sew.

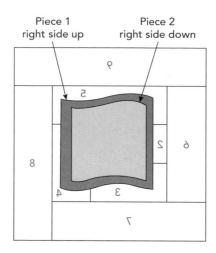

FABRIC SIDE
Fabric pieces 1 and 2 in position

6. Turn the foundation to the Printed Side and sew the seamline between pieces 1 and 2. Your seamline should be ¼″ longer than the line at each side, extending into an adjacent piece at each end. (This extended seamline will be covered by fabric pieces that you will add later.) I prefer to backstitch or use a lock stitch at the beginning and end of each line of stitching, though you may choose not to.

Use a small stitch (15–20 per inch) to simplify paper removal once the quilt top is assembled.

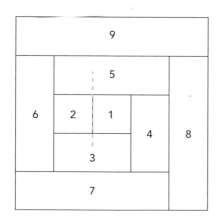

PRINTED SIDE
Extended seam sewn between pieces 1 and 2

7. Trim the seam allowances to approximately ¼″ (eyeball the distance). Press to set the seam.

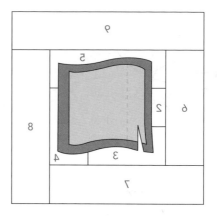

FABRIC SIDE
Trim seam allowances, then press.

8. Flip piece 2 so that it covers numbered space 2 on the foundation. Press.

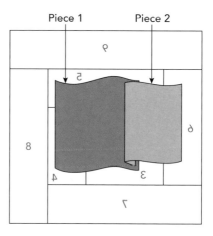

FABRIC SIDE
Press piece 2 into place.

NOTE: I press twice, once to "set the seam" before flipping the piece (Step 7) and then again after piece 2 is flipped into place (Step 8). Setting the seam makes the seamline straight. It isn't time wasted.

9. Add each piece according to the numbered sequence until the entire foundation is covered.

10. Trim the seam allowances along the outside edges of the block to ¼″.

GENERAL TIPS

The following are a few general tips that routinely apply to paper foundation piecing—especially to Flip-Flop Paper Piecing. These tips will not be repeated throughout the next fourteen chapters. However, they will, in every case, make block construction easier, more accurate, or more successful:

Tip 1: Choose fabrics that are thin and crisp. Avoid upholstery, home decor, and even high-quality quilt fabric composed of fat threads.

Tip 2: Choose fabrics that are opaque (that is, that are not see-through).

NOTE: If you really, really must use a pale, transparent yellow fabric over a black one, either interface the yellow fabric or be careful in trimming the seams to prevent the black fabric seam allowance from showing through the yellow fabric.

Tip 3: Always use starch or spray sizing while pressing your fabric before you cut it. The heavier the starch or sizing, the better. In my opinion, fabric cannot be too stiff.

Tip 4: Draft paper foundations without a ¼" seam allowance around the outer edges of the blocks. Maybe it's just my hands, but I find blocks easier to pin and sew together without the foundation paper in the seam allowances. To add stability as I sew, however, I always slip a piece of ordinary notebook paper under the pieces I'm sewing if I begin, end, or completely sew a seam in an unpapered seam allowance.

IMPORTANT: When you finish paper piecing a block and are ready to trim off the raggedy edges, add a ¼" seam allowance all along the outside edge of the paper foundation. Do *not* trim even with the edge of the paper foundation. The patterns presented in this book include the outside edge seam allowance to remind you of this important step.

Tip 5: On every paper foundation, indicate which fabric is to be placed on each numbered piece. Because you will be working in reverse, it is amazingly easy to sew the wrong fabric onto a numbered space. I use a colored pencil or washable marker to mark each numbered space with the color of the fabric to be placed there. Just a quick swipe of color will do;

you don't have to color the entire space. If more than one fabric has the same color, use the appropriately colored pencil or marker to write a key word, such as "stripe" or "flower".

Tip 6: On every paper foundation, indicate which seams are "green legs" and which are "red." (I promise that this will make sense after you read Chapter 2.) I use a swipe of green washable highlighter to mark the green leg of each flip-flopped piece. The unmarked leg would then be the red leg.

Tip 7: Use sharp/jeans or quilting sewing machine needles. Many quilters prefer a large sharp/jeans needle (90/14 or 100/16) for ease in later paper removal, but I prefer an 80/12 sharp/jeans needle or a 75/11 quilting needle for sewing a straight, crisp line and for producing smaller puncture holes in fabric.

Tip 8: Use a single-hole throat plate if you have one. If you don't have one, buy one. You'll never regret it.

Tip 9: Always use an open-toe embroidery foot, as this allows you to clearly see the lines on which you will sew.

Tip 10: When marking lines directly on your fabric, use fabric markers that are both washable and incapable of being heat set by an iron. I use chalk markers or air-erasable markers. Testing is always the safest approach.

Tip 11: Trim each seam allowance as you progress from step to step in Flip-Flop Foundation Piecing, just as you would in traditional foundation piecing (pages 9–10). It's easier and more accurate to use scissors, rather than a rotary cutter, for trimming.

Tip 12: When the block is complete, trim each block's outside seam allowance to ¼". Do **not** trim the fabric flush with the paper foundation unless the seam allowance was added to the foundation pattern.

Tip 13: Wait to remove paper foundations until all the blocks are joined into a quilt top.

Tip 14: Enlarge or reduce the patterns to make a different-size block. Each pattern is sized for a 2¼" block or a 6" block. Reduce the 6" pattern by photocopying at 50% for a 3" block or at 25% for a 1½" block. If you change the size of the patterns, use a ruler to properly readjust the outside seam allowances to ¼".

TRADITIONAL FOUNDATION PIECING VERSUS FLIP-FLOP FOUNDATION PIECING

In traditional foundation piecing, all the sewing is done on the Printed Side of the foundation. In Flip-Flop Paper Piecing, the sewing is done on both the Printed and the Fabric sides. The foundation will be flipped back and forth, back and forth (flip-flop, flip-flop—hence the name) as seams are sewn first on one side (the Printed Side) and then on the other (the unprinted Fabric Side).

To construct the Birds in the Air block using traditional foundation piecing, you would need two foundations. Foundation A and Foundation B would each be constructed with a seam allowance along all edges. Then Foundation A would be sewn to Foundation B, carefully matching each point, as well as the beginning and ending of each seam. I hate that part.

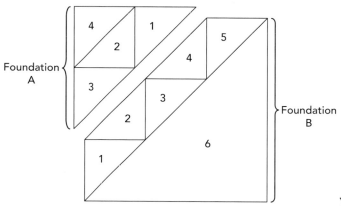

Two foundations needed for traditional foundation piecing

Flip-Flop Paper Piecing enables the quilter to quickly, accurately, and miraculously piece Birds in the Air on a single foundation, eliminating the miserable job of sewing together multiple foundations to complete just one block.

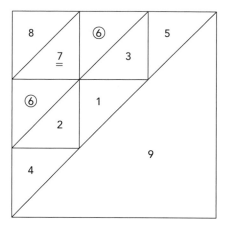

One foundation needed for Flip-Flop Paper Piecing

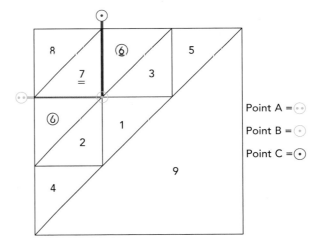

CODED INSTRUCTIONS

The instructions for constructing each flip-flop foundation-pieced block are coded using numbers, symbols, colored lines, and dots on the foundation itself. As in traditional foundation piecing, the construction sequence of each piece on the block is indicated by numbers. The other lines, dots, and symbols give the flip-flop quilter other essential information:

- The circled numbers show which pieces of the block are constructed simultaneously.

- The numbers marked with a double line show which pieces have one segment or leg first sewn on the Printed Side and then the second segment or leg sewn from the unprinted Fabric Side. These pieces are called flip-flop pieces. The first leg is highlighted in green for "Go." The second leg is highlighted in red for "Stop and wait a minute; you come second."

If you want to Flip-Flop Paper Piece blocks not included in this book, please see the valuable information in the Appendix (page 93) to help you decide which leg to sew first.

Coded foundation

Point A = ⊙⊙
Point B = ⊙
Point C = ⊙

This color-coded information will make much more sense as you read through the instructions for each block.

To help you follow the instructions, the illustrations will show the numbers reversed when the Printed Side is shown face down.

The scale used for the instructional illustrations shown throughout the book is based on the 2¼" finished block.

The Basic Flip-Flop

(Birds in the Air and The Four Knaves)

INTRODUCTION

The instructions for Birds in the Air are coded in the illustrations. This coding may mean nothing to you at this point. However, if you follow the simple step-by-step block construction instructions, it will all make sense.

The numbers on the foundation pattern indicate the sequence of construction. The circled number 6 indicates that these pieces are constructed simultaneously. The double line under number 7 tells us that this is the flip-flop piece. Piece 7 has two legs: The leg highlighted in green is sewn first on the Printed Side, stopping precisely at Point B. The leg highlighted in red is fused or sewn last from the unprinted Fabric Side.

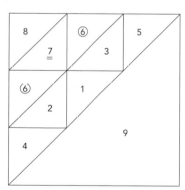

Foundation with Instructions

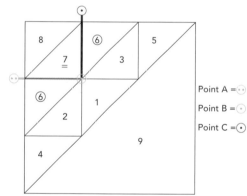

Highlighted Instructional Block

Point A = (··)
Point B = (·)
Point C = (·)

Completed Block: Birds in the Air

BIRDS IN THE AIR BLOCK CONSTRUCTION

Unless otherwise specified, your stitched seamline should be ¼" longer than the printed line at each side, extending into an adjacent piece at each end.

1. Sew pieces 1–5 just as you would in traditional foundation piecing (pages 9–10). *Fabric is placed on the unprinted Fabric Side. Seams are sewn on the Printed Side.*

2. Cut a single piece of fabric large enough to cover both pieces 6 and 6 and the space between them.

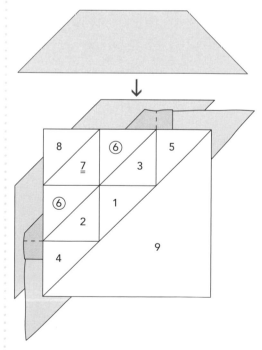

Cut fabric to cover both pieces 6 and 6.

3. Place the single, large piece of fabric from Step 2 right side down on the Fabric Side. Sew on the Printed Side just as in traditional foundation piecing. The only difference is that the fabric will cover more than one piece at the same time. Sew both 6 pieces simultaneously.

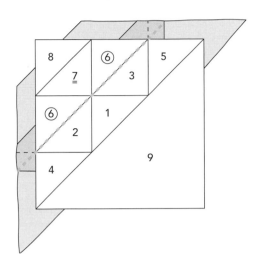

Sew and press large piece 6 and 6 into place.

4. Place flip-flop piece 7 right side down on the unprinted Fabric Side of the foundation. Align the piece so that you can sew the first leg (highlighted in green on the Highlighted Instructional Block).

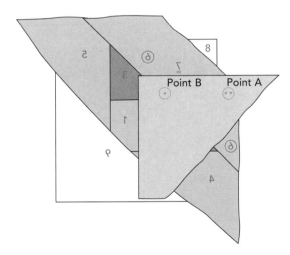

Place piece 7 right side down.

5. Sew the green leg first. On the Printed Side, start stitching at Point A in the seam allowance and stop precisely at Point B (at the tip of the triangular piece being sewn). *Backstitch or lock stitch at Point B.* Open piece 7 into place.

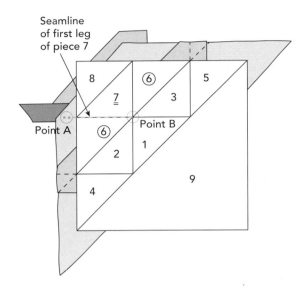

Sew first leg of piece 7 and open.

6. The following technique for finishing the second leg of piece 7 is the key to Flip-Flop Paper Piecing. Important: You will flip the foundation and work on the unprinted Fabric Side, not on the Printed Side.

a. Turn the foundation to the Fabric Side and press piece 7 into place. At this stage of construction, flip-flop piece 7 is sewn only from Point A to Point B and pressed into place with the raw edge of the seam allowance on the left side.

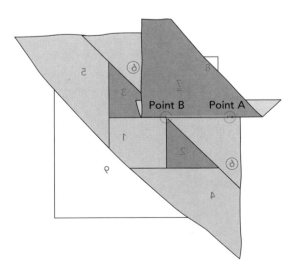

Press piece 7 into place.

b. Insert pins at Points B and C to mark the seamline for the second leg (highlighted in red on the Highlighted Instructional Block). Go straight up from the Printed Side, where Points B and C are clearly visible, through to the unprinted Fabric Side.

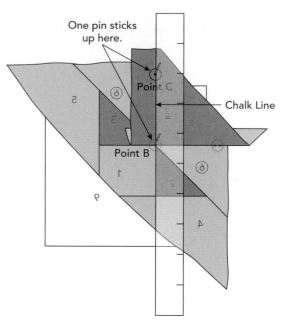

One pin sticks up here.

Point C

Chalk Line

Point B

Place ruler along seamline from Point B through Point C and draw line.

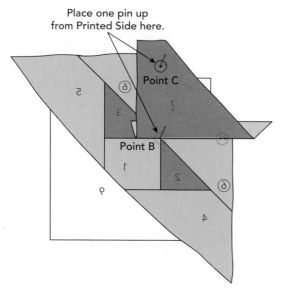

Place one pin up from Printed Side here.

Point C

Point B

FABRIC SIDE
Place pins at Points B and C.

c. Place a thin, see-through ruler over piece 7, from Point B through Point C, using the pins as your guideline. Note that the ruler also goes straight along the seamline of piece 2. Draw a line from Point B through Point C to mark the seamline for the second leg. Remove the pins.

NOTE: Be sure the marker you use is washable and incapable of being heat set by an iron. I use a chalk or air-erasable marker. (Testing is always the safest approach.)

d. Trim the seam allowance for this newly marked seamline to approximately ¼". I just eyeball this measurement, but if your standards are stricter, you could measure, mark, and then trim. Whether you eyeball it or precision cut it, be sure to trim only piece 7 and not the underlying piece 6.

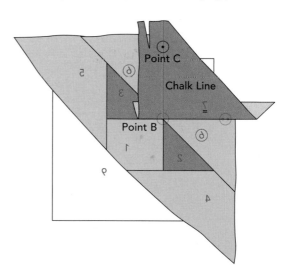

Point C

Chalk Line

Point B

Trim seam allowance to approximately $1/4$".

e. Turn back piece 7, exposing its wrong side.

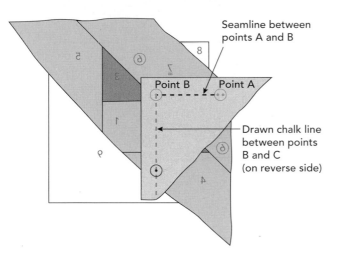

Turn back piece 7.

f. Press the seam allowance along the marked chalk line. Trim one layer of the seam allowance at an angle to reduce bulk.

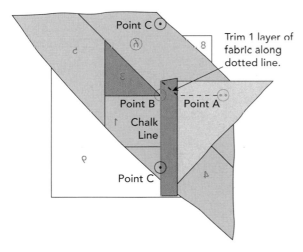

Press seam allowance along chalk line.

g. Fold the corner of the seam allowance at Point B diagonally and press. Be sure to include as much of the seam allowance as possible.

NOTE: I use an awl or a wooden cuticle stick for maximum folding power.

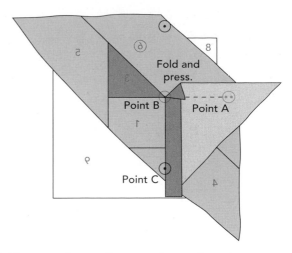

Fold corner of seam allowance diagonally and press.

h. Complete the second leg of flip-flop piece 7. You have three options for completing the seamline along the second leg of all flip-flop pieces. Whichever option you choose, reinsert pins at Points B and C (as in Step 6b) to ensure that the flip-flop piece is accurately positioned when pressed into position.

Option 1: Hand Sew the Seam

Press the piece into its final position and hand stitch, using a needle and thread. Begin in the seam allowance at Point C and end at Point B, shown with the red dotted line in the illustration. If you plan to hand quilt your finished quilt, this option is probably the best choice.

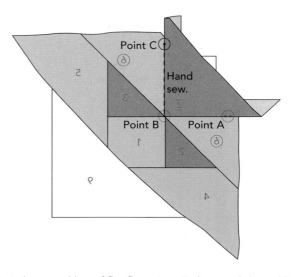

Hand stitch second leg of flip-flop piece 7 along red dotted line.

Option 2: Blind-Hem or Zigzag Stitch the Seam by Machine

Press piece 7 into its final position, securing it with a single pin at the Point C end.

Set your machine to blind-hem or zigzag stitch, thread it with invisible monofilament thread (or a lightweight matching thread), and sew the seam into place, beginning at Point B and ending at Point C.

If you just barely catch piece 7 with each zigzag stitch, this seam, although sewn from the Fabric Side of the foundation, will be almost invisible.

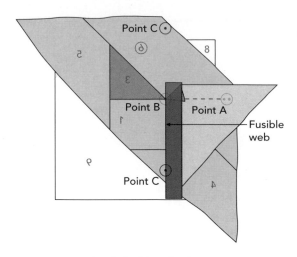

Apply fusible adhesive.

Fold piece 7 into its final position and follow the manufacturer's directions to iron the fusible adhesive permanently into place.

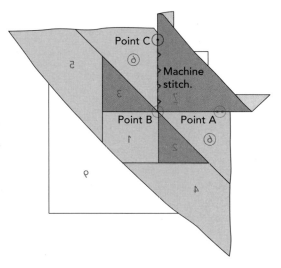

Machine blind-hem or zigzag stitch second leg of flip-flop piece 7 along red dotted line.

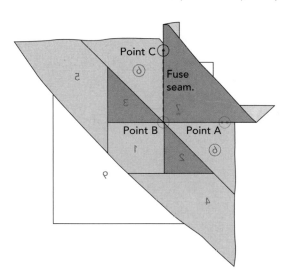

Fuse second leg of flip-flop piece 7 into place along red dotted line.

Option 3: Fuse the Seam into Place

Fuse the seam into place with a ¼" strip of fusible web. I use Regular (not Lite) Steam-A-Seam 2 sold in ¼"-wide rolls. If you choose this option, iron-tack the fusible web to the seam at the end of Step 6g (page 17).

Be generous as you attach the fusible adhesive strip. Apply the strip as illustrated, going past Point B ⅛"–¼" into the space that piece 7 will soon occupy. Once the fusible web is iron-tacked in place, you can remove the paper backing from the adhesive.

This option is my personal favorite. It may not be the best choice if your quilt will receive heavy use and frequent laundering, as in a drag-along child's quilt. In most cases, however, it should be just fine, especially if the fused seams are reinforced in the quilting phase. See the illustrations for ideas.

7. Sew pieces 8 and 9 as you would in traditional foundation piecing.

8. Smile. You now have a block with perfectly matched points, a block whose final size is exactly the size you originally chose. Success!

QUILTING SUGGESTIONS FOR BLOCKS WITH FUSED SEAMS

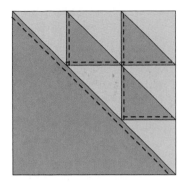

Quilt lines following fused seamlines

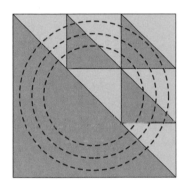

Quilt lines crossing over fused seamlines

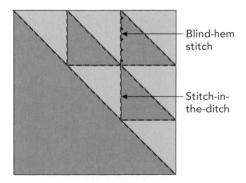

Blind-hem stitch

Stitch-in-the-ditch

Quilt lines stitched in the ditch with monofilament thread and sneaky blind-hem stitch

The sneaky blind-hem stitch is my favorite approach for quilting. I just love pieced patchwork quilted exclusively in-the-ditch style, so that no visible quilting mars the beautiful geometric patchwork. I drop the

feed dogs, thread the machine with monofilament thread, and fill the bobbin with a lightweight cotton thread (#60 or #100). Next, I free-motion stitch in the ditch around every piece in each block. When I stitch along a previously fused seam, I just catch a very small bite of the fabric on that fused seam every three to five stitches. This reinforcement of the fused line may or may not be absolutely necessary, but I am nothing if not compulsive.

PRACTICE YOUR SKILLS: THE FOUR KNAVES

If you have mastered the technique and learned the meaning of the symbols used in constructing Birds in the Air, you should be ready to complete The Four Knaves by following only the diagrammed instructions below. If you need a bit of a refresher on technique or symbols, refer to the previous detailed directions.

You will cut four pieces as single, large pieces of fabric that will cover two triangles plus the space between them (2 and 2, 3 and 3, 4 and 4, and 5 and 5). Four basic flip-flop pieces (pieces 6–9) will be sewn green leg first from the Printed Side and then sewn (or fused) red leg second from the unprinted Fabric Side.

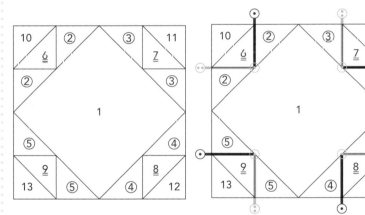

Point A = ⊙
Point B = ⊙
Point C = ⊙

Foundation with Instructions   Highlighted Instructional Block

Completed Block: The Four Knaves

Birds in the Air

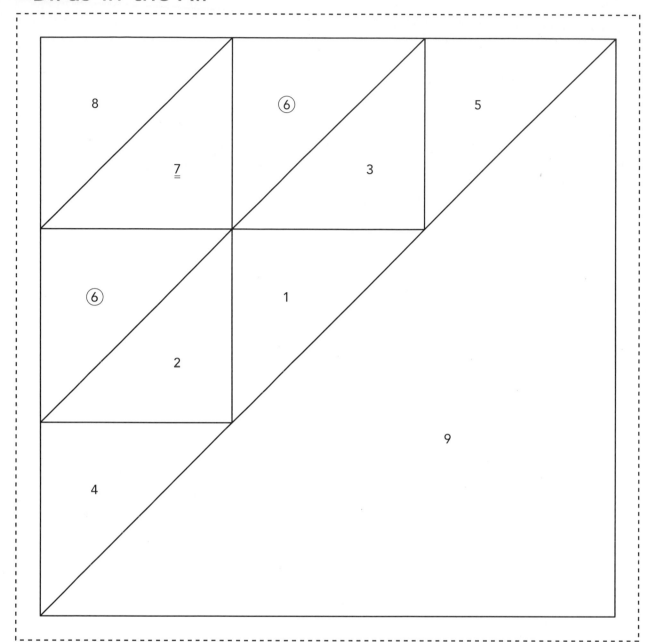

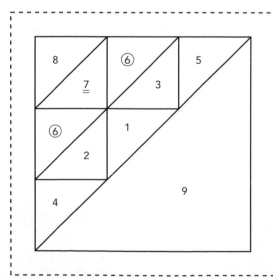

Birds in the Air

The Four Knaves

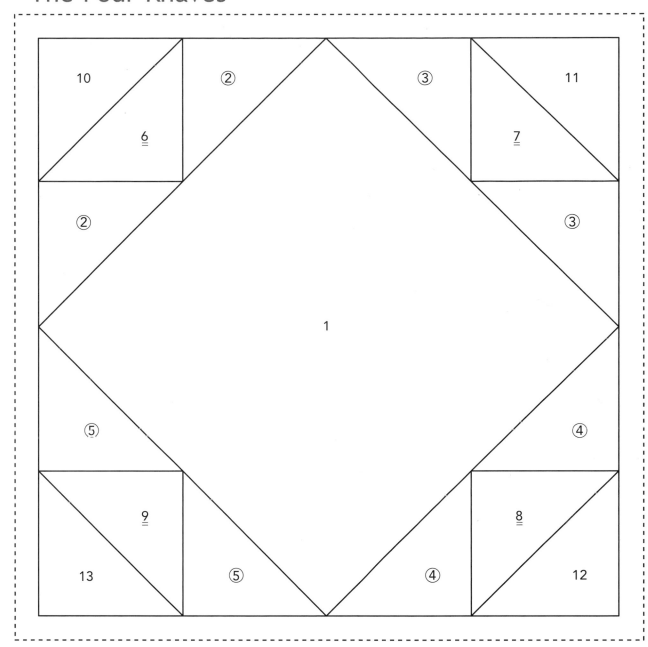

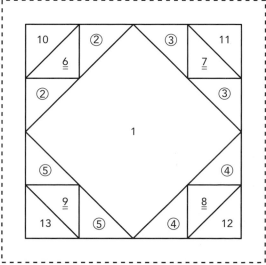

3 Say Goodbye to the Y
(Attic Window and Jewel)

INTRODUCTION

The Attic Window block contains the classic—and often dreaded—Y-seam. But fear not—Flip-Flop Paper Piecing will eliminate that pesky Y and produce a sharp, classic 45° seam good enough to satisfy anyone, even should the quilt police arrive with rulers in hand.

The numbers on the foundation indicate the sequence of construction. The double line under number 3 tells us that this is the flip-flop piece. It has two legs: The leg highlighted in green is sewn first on the Printed Side, stopping precisely at Point B. The leg highlighted in red is fused or sewn last from the unprinted Fabric Side.

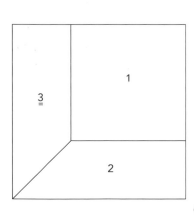

Foundation with Instructions

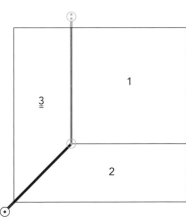

Highlighted Instructional Block

Point A = ⦿
Point B = ⊙
Point C = ⊙

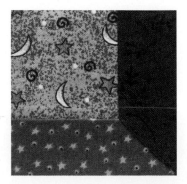

Completed Block: Attic Window

ATTIC WINDOW BLOCK CONSTRUCTION

Unless otherwise specified, your stitched seamline should be ¼" longer than the printed line at each side, extending into an adjacent piece at each end.

1. Sew pieces 1 and 2 as you would in traditional foundation piecing (pages 9–10). *All fabric is placed on the unprinted Fabric Side. Seams are sewn on the Printed Side.*

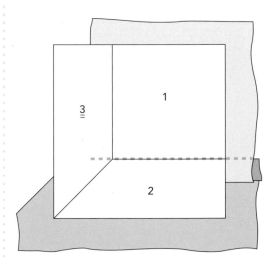

Sew extended line between pieces 1 and 2 (viewed from Printed Side).

2. Place flip-flop piece 3 right side down on the unprinted Fabric Side of the foundation. Align the piece so that the first leg (highlighted in green on the Highlighted Instructional Block) can be sewn. Start stitching at Point A in the seam allowance and stop precisely at Point B.

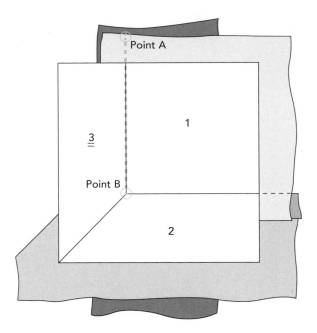

Sew first leg of piece 3.

b. Insert pins at Points B and C to mark the seamline for the second leg (highlighted in red on the Highlighted Instructional Block). Go straight up from the Printed Side, where Points B and C are clearly visible, through to the unprinted Fabric Side.

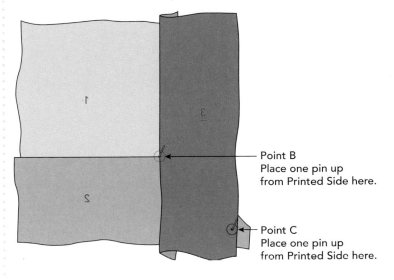

Point B
Place one pin up
from Printed Side here.

Point C
Place one pin up
from Printed Side here.

FABRIC SIDE
Place pins at Points B and C.

3. The following technique for finishing the second leg of piece 3 is the key to Flip-Flop Paper Piecing. Important: You will flip the foundation and work on the unprinted Fabric Side, not on the Printed Side.

a. Turn the foundation to the Fabric Side and press piece 3 into place.

c. Place a thin, see-through ruler over piece 3, from Point B through Point C, using the pins as your guideline. Draw a line from Point B through Point C to mark the seamline for the second leg. Be sure to use a marker that is washable and incapable of being heat set by an iron. Remove the pins.

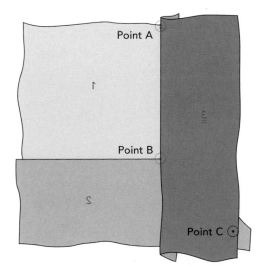

Press piece 3 into place.

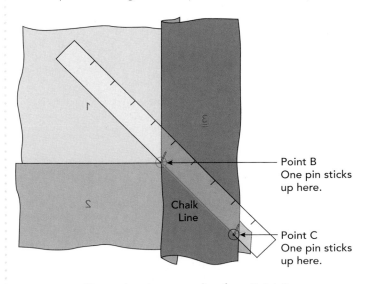

Point B
One pin sticks
up here.

Chalk
Line

Point C
One pin sticks
up here.

Place ruler along seamline from Point B
through Point C and draw line.

d. Trim the seam allowance for this newly marked seamline to approximately ¼". Be sure to trim only piece 3 and not the underlying piece 2.

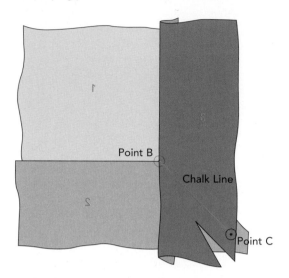

Trim seam allowance to ¼".

e. Turn back piece 3, exposing its wrong side.

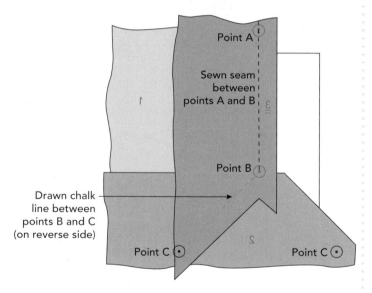

Turn back piece 3.

f. Press the seam allowance along the marked chalk line. Trim one layer of the seam allowance at an angle to reduce bulk.

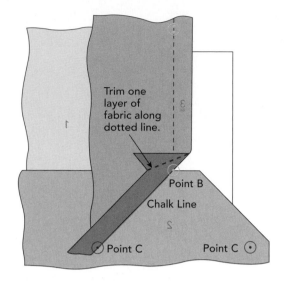

Press seam allowance along chalk line.

g. To create a guide for correct placement, reinsert a pin at Point C, going up from the Printed Side straight through to the Fabric Side. Complete the second leg of piece 3 by hand sewing, using the machine blind-hem (or zigzag) stitch, or fusing (pages 17–18). Whichever option you choose, piece 3 will be pressed into its final position, a perfect 45° angle on a block that is exactly the size it is supposed to be.

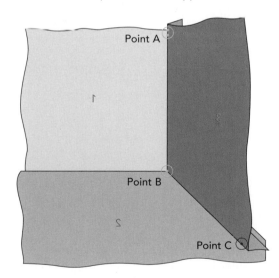

Press piece 3, then sew or fuse into place.

h. Smirk. You have a perfect block, and you knew you would, even before you started.

PRACTICE YOUR SKILLS: JEWEL

The following block, a variation of the traditional Jewel block, has four Y's for an extra-special Y-seam workout. Just as in Attic Windows, in this block, the Y will be eliminated by a simple flip-flop maneuver: Sew the green leg on the Printed Side, stopping at Point B. Next, sew or fuse the red leg from the Fabric Side.

Goodbye Y and good riddance!

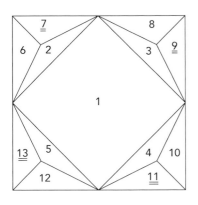

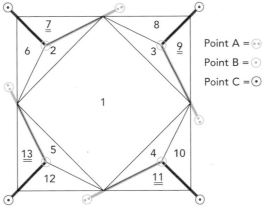

Point A = (⊙⊙)
Point B = (⊙)
Point C = ⊙

Foundation with Instructions   Highlighted Instructional Block

Completed Block: Jewel

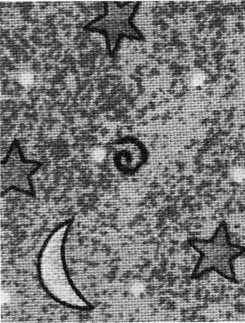

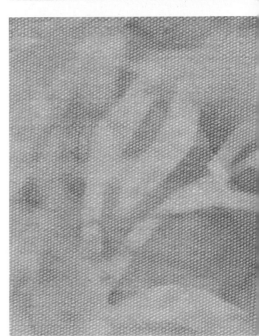

Attic Window

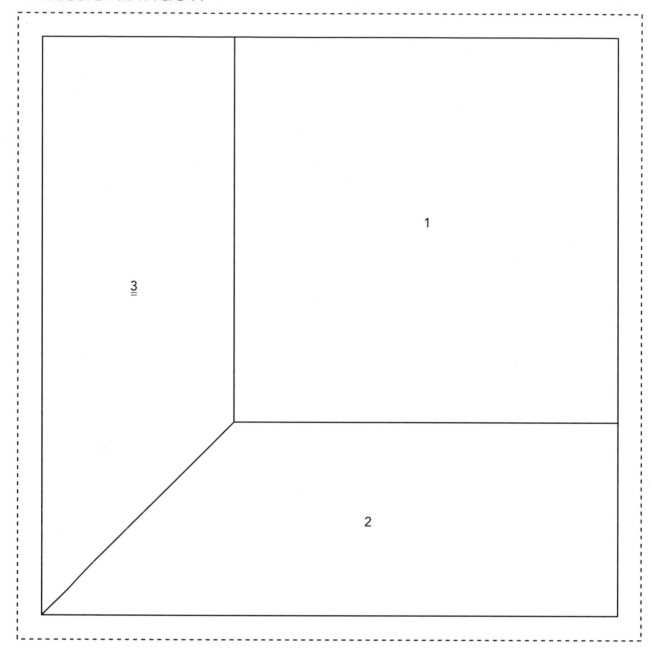

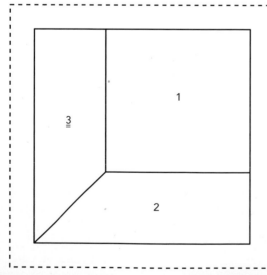

Jewel

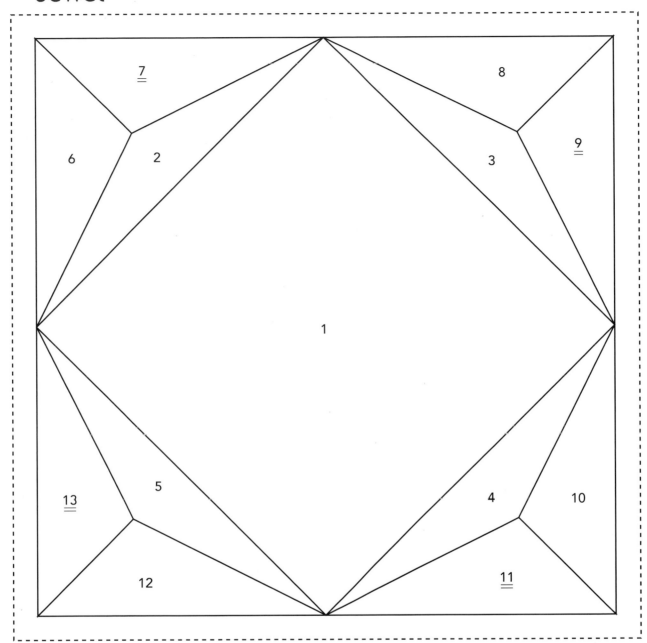

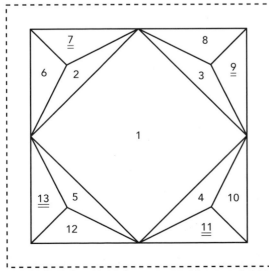

4 When Seams Collide
(Churn Dash and Alaska Homestead)

INTRODUCTION

The earliest steps in a flip-flop paper-pieced block may sometimes appear to be the same as those in traditional foundation piecing but may actually differ slightly in construction. A small adjustment is occasionally needed to prevent the seam allowance of one piece from colliding into that of another. Churn Dash presents an example of the modification that needs to be made to avoid a dangerous head-on collision. This technique is simple: Just stop at the stop sign.

The numbers on the foundation represent the sequence of construction. The stop signs around pieces 2–5 indicate that these pieces will be sewn from one Point B to the other Point B. You will stop just as if there were stop signs at these intersections. Think of it as sewing from dot to dot, starting and stopping precisely at the ends of a seam. The double lines under numbers 10–13 indicate that these are flip-flopped pieces that will be sewn in two segments (legs). The leg highlighted in green is sewn first from the Printed Side. The leg highlighted in red is sewn or fused second from the Fabric Side.

CHURN DASH BLOCK CONSTRUCTION

Unless otherwise specified, your stitched seamline should be ¼" longer than the printed line at each side, extending into an adjacent piece at each end.

1. Place piece 1 right side up on the unprinted Fabric Side. Place piece 2 right side down on top of piece 1.

2. On the Printed Side, sew the seam between pieces 1 and 2 from one Point B to the next Point B. Obey the stop sign and *sew from point to point only*, just as if there were a stop sign at each Point B intersection. *Do not* extend the stitching into the adjacent pieces. Press.

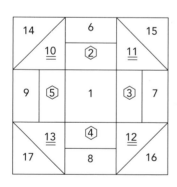

Foundation with Instructions

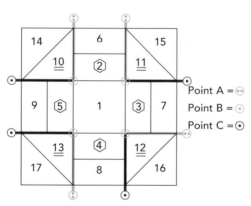

Point A = ⊙⊙
Point B = ⊙
Point C = ⊙

Highlighted Instructional Block

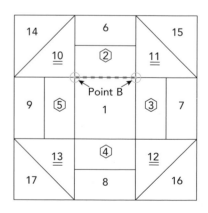

PRINTED SIDE

Completed Block: Churn Dash

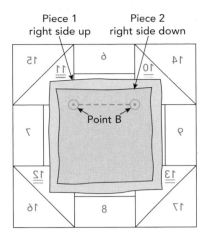

Piece 1
right side up

Piece 2
right side down

Point B

FABRIC SIDE
Sew seam between pieces 1 and 2
from one Point B to next Point B.

3. Sew pieces 3–5 exactly as you sewed piece 2 (Step 2), starting and stopping precisely at each Point B. Be sure to press each piece open before you attach the next piece.

TIP: Press firmly along the seamline to avoid the "fatal fold," a fold of fabric that can form along the seamline and destroy foundation-piecing perfection. To prevent the fold from re-forming, use a silk-weight pin to hold the pressed piece in place on the paper foundation until the piece is sewn down.

4. Sew pieces 6–9 just as you would in traditional foundation piecing (pages 9–10).

5. Before sewing the first leg of flip-flop piece 10, note that the seam allowance produced in Step 3 (when piece 5 was sewn to piece 1) appears to be in the way. We must avoid a head-on collision, this time between the seam we are about to sew (piece 10 to pieces 6 and 2) and a previously sewn seam (piece 5 to piece 1).

The solution is simple. Just pin the interfering seam allowance out of the way. I scoot it with a cuticle stick or awl and pin it down with a silk-weight pin. As I pin it, a little rhyme runs through my head to remind me of what I need to do: "When seams collide, pin one aside."

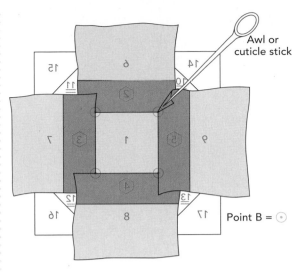

Awl or
cuticle stick

Point B = ⊙

Before attaching first leg of piece 10, pull aside
and then pin seam allowance of piece 5.

Once that pesky seam allowance is pinned aside, the way is clear for the first leg of flip-flop piece 10 to be sewn.

6. Place fabric piece 10 right side down on the unprinted Fabric Side of the foundation. Align the piece so that you can sew the first leg (highlighted in green on the Highlighted Instructional Block).

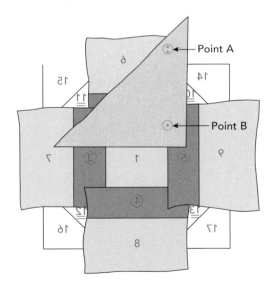

Point A

Point B

Place piece 10 right side down on Fabric Side.

7. Sew the green leg first. Start stitching at Point A in the seam allowance and stop precisely at Point B.

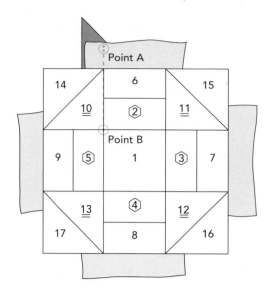

Sew first leg of piece 10 from Point A to Point B.

8. The following technique for finishing the second leg of piece 10 is the key to Flip-Flop Paper Piecing. Important: You will flip the foundation and work on the unprinted Fabric Side, not on the Printed Side.

a. Turn the foundation to the Fabric Side, remove the pin holding aside the seam allowance of piece 5, and press the seam allowance back into place. I use a cuticle stick or awl to pull it back down, shove it around, and smooth it into place. This requires a bit of tugging, because there will seem to be too much fabric in too little space. I pull from the underside of the seam allowance to smooth it right into its proper position.

b. Press piece 10 into place.

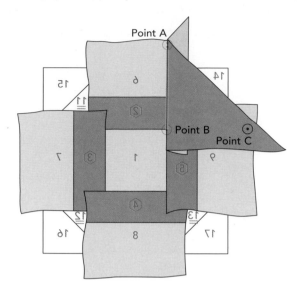

Press piece 10 into place.

c. Insert pins at Points B and C to mark the seamline for the second leg (highlighted in red on the Highlighted Instructional Block). Go straight up from the Printed Side, where Points B and C are clearly visible, through to the unprinted Fabric Side.

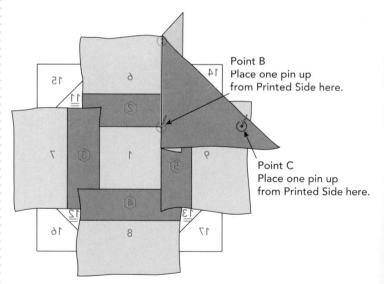

FABRIC SIDE
Place pins at Points B and C.

d. Place a thin, see-through ruler over piece 10, from Point B through Point C, using the pins as your guideline. Note that the ruler also goes straight along the lower seamline of piece 2. Draw a line from Point B through Point C to mark the seamline for the second leg. Be sure to use a marker that is washable and incapable of being heat set by an iron. Remove the pins.

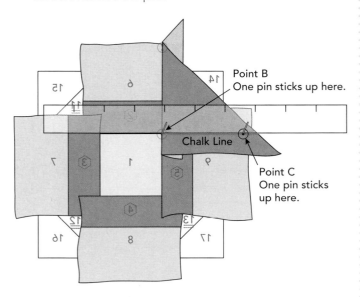

Place ruler along seamline from Point B through Point C and draw line.

e. Trim the seam allowance for this newly marked seamline to approximately ¼". Be sure to trim only piece 10 and not the underlying pieces 9 and 5.

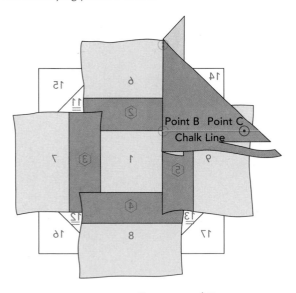

Trim seam allowance to ¼".

f. Turn back piece 10, exposing its wrong side.

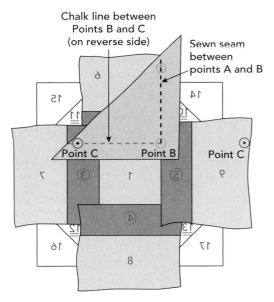

Turn back piece 10.

g. Press the seam allowance along the marked chalk line. Trim one layer of the seam allowance at an angle to reduce bulk.

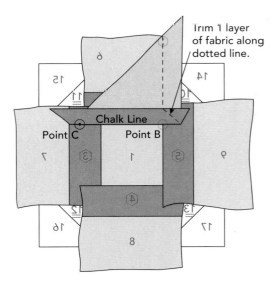

Press seam allowance along chalk line.

h. Fold the corner of the seam allowance at Point B diagonally and press. Be sure to include as much of the seam allowance as possible.

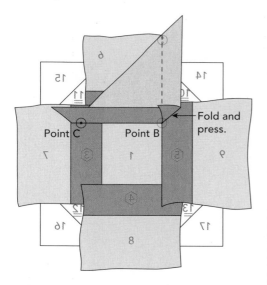

Fold corner of seam allowance diagonally and press.

i. Complete the second leg of piece 10 by hand sewing, using the machine blind-hem (or zigzag) stitch, or fusing (pages 17–18). Whichever option you choose, press flip-flop piece 10 and then secure it into its final position—a thing of beauty in a world that needs all the beauty it can get.

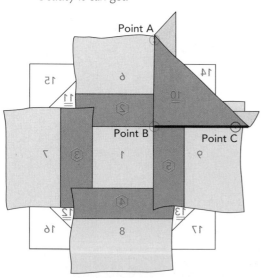

Press second leg of piece 10 into place, then sew or fuse.

9. Sew flip-flop pieces 11–13 exactly as you sewed piece 10.

10. Sew pieces 14–17 as you would in traditional foundation piecing.

PRACTICE YOUR SKILLS: ALASKA HOMESTEAD

The following Alaska Homestead block has four B points at which the seams collide. All will be well if you stop at those Point B stop signs as you sew pieces 2–5. Then pin the colliding seam allowances aside as you sew the first green leg on pieces 10–13.

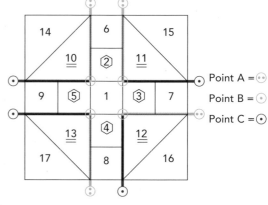

Foundation with Instructions   Highlighted Instructional Block

Point A = ⊙⊙
Point B = ⊙
Point C = ⊙

Completed Block: Alaska Homestead

Churn Dash

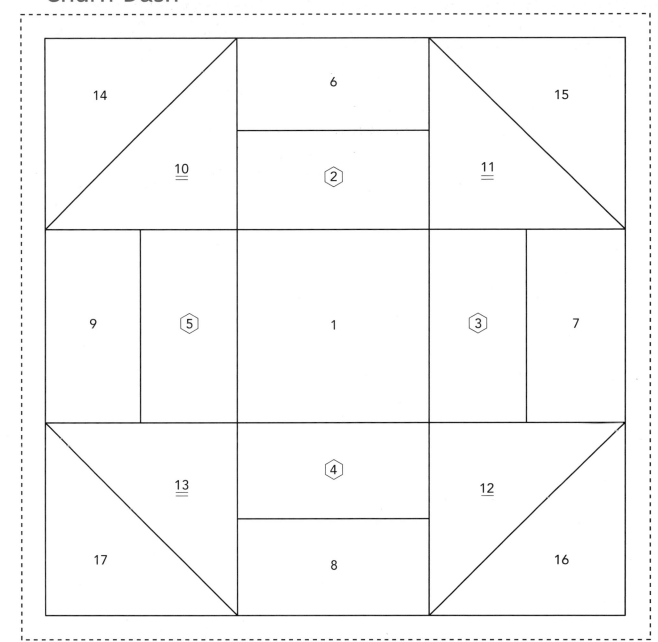

14	6	15
10	2	11
9 5	1	3 7
13	4	12
17	8	16

Alaska Homestead

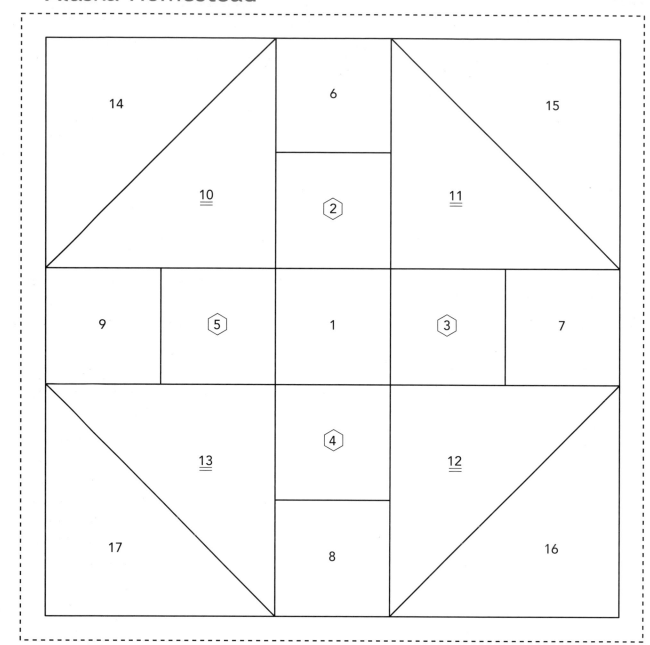

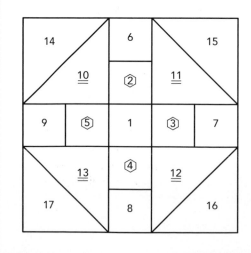

5 Shoot from the Corner

(Sawtooth and Delectable Mountain)

INTRODUCTION

Many pieced blocks are constructed with a sawtooth edge going around a center square or half square. Traditional examples would be Bear Tracks, Maple Leaf, Duck's Foot in the Mud, Kansas Troubles, and on and on.

It is no easy task to make all the little triangles in these blocks the same size, the same angle, and all sharply defined with no cut-off points and no floating points. No easy task, that is, unless you Flip-Flop Paper Piece the block. Then it is a joy.

Starting at the corner (piece 1) and going out toward each end provides a raw-edge-free surface at Point B for the application of flip-flop piece 13. This piecing method also produces symmetry among the sawtooth points.

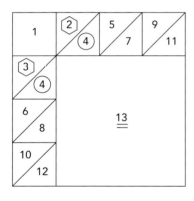

Foundation with Instructions

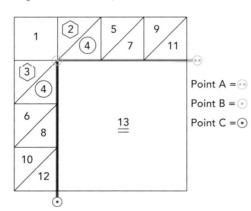

Highlighted Instructional Block

Point A = ⊙⊙
Point B = ⊙
Point C = ⊙

Completed Block: Sawtooth

SAWTOOTH BLOCK CONSTRUCTION

Unless otherwise specified, your stitched seamline should be ¼" longer than the printed line at each side, extending into an adjacent piece at each end.

1. Place piece 1 right side up on the unprinted Fabric Side. Place piece 2 right side down on top of piece 1.

2. On the Printed Side, sew the seam between pieces 1 and 2, beginning in the outer seam allowance. Because piece 2 is encircled by a stop sign, do not continue into the adjacent piece at the other end. Stop precisely at Point B (the stop sign). Then press that piece into place.

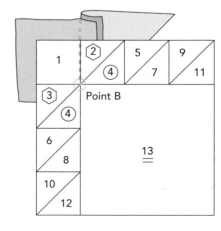

PRINTED SIDE
Sew seam between pieces 1 and 2
to Point B, then press.

3. Pin or press piece 2 out of the way, so you do not sew over it. Sew piece 3 to piece 1, obeying the stop sign. Sew exactly as you did piece 2, starting in the seam allowance and stopping precisely at Point B.

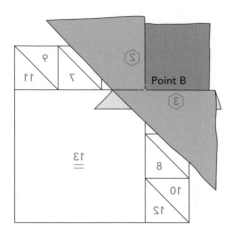

Sew piece 3 to piece 1, stopping at Point B.

4. Cut a single piece of fabric large enough to cover both pieces 4 and 4 and the space between them.

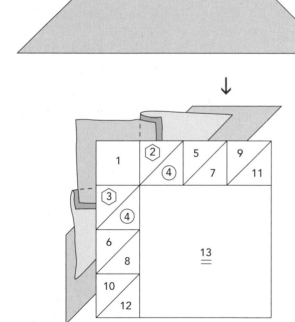

Cut fabric to cover both 4 and 4.

> **TIP:** In Step 9, to avoid the appearance of chopped-off points, sew one thread away from those points as you foundation piece on the Printed Side. Sewing barely off the line will let those points shine.

5. Place the single, large piece of fabric from Step 4 right side down on the Fabric Side.

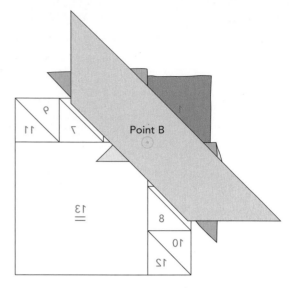

Place large piece 4 and 4 right side down.

6. On the Printed Side, sew large piece 4 and 4 to both pieces 2 and 3 simultaneously, crossing exactly through Point B. Press. This large piece of fabric will provide a smooth, clean surface for attaching the flip-flop piece 13.

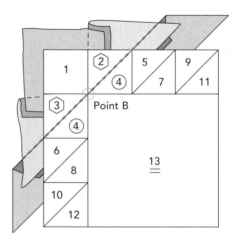

Sew and press large piece 4 and 4.

7. Trim off all the previously produced seam allowances underneath piece 4.

8. Sew pieces 5–12 just as you would in traditional foundation piecing (pages 9–10). Trim the interior seam allowances to ¼". Be careful not to trim any closer than ⅛" because you will be adding flip-flop piece 13 along these edges.

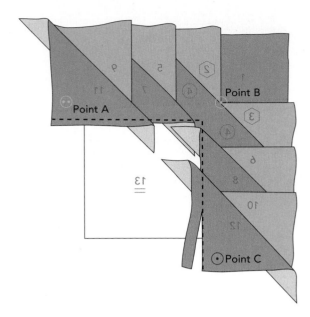

Sew pieces 5–12 and trim seam allowance.

9. Place flip-flop piece 13 right side down on the unprinted Fabric Side of the foundation. Align the piece so you can sew the first leg (highlighted in green on the Highlighted Instructional Block). Start stitching at Point A at the edge of the seam allowance and stop precisely at Point B. Because you prepared a lovely, smooth surface when adding pieces 4 and 4, no seam allowance needs to be pinned aside.

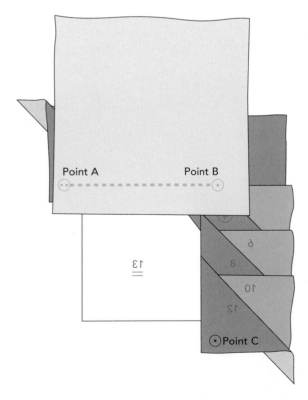

Place piece 13 right side down and sew from Point A to Point B.

10. The following technique for finishing the second leg of piece 13 is the key to Flip-Flop Foundation Piecing. Important: You will flip the foundation and work on the unprinted Fabric Side, not on the Printed Side.

a. Turn the foundation to the Fabric Side and press piece 13 into place.

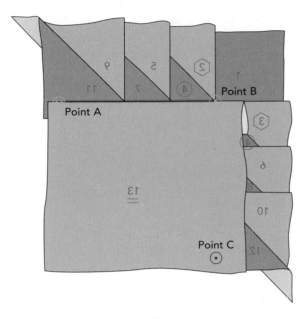

Press piece 13 into place.

b. Insert pins at Points B and C to mark the seamline for the second leg (highlighted in red on the Highlighted Instructional Block). Go straight up from the Printed Side, where Points B and C are clearly visible, through to the unprinted Fabric Side.

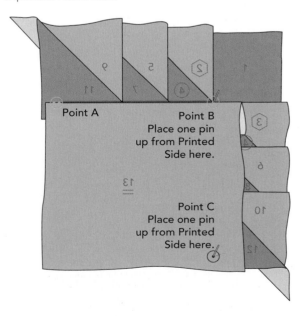

FABRIC SIDE
Place pins at Points B and C.

c. Place a thin, see-through ruler over piece 13, from Point B through Point C, using the pins as your guideline. Note that the ruler goes straight along the seamline of piece 1. Draw a line from Point B through Point C to mark the seamline for the second leg. Be sure to use a marker that is washable and incapable of being heat set by an iron. Remove the pins.

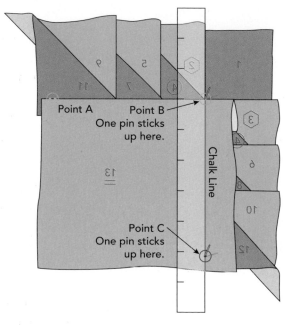

Place ruler along seamline from Point B through Point C and draw line.

d. Trim the seam allowance for this newly marked seam to approximately ¼". Be sure to trim only piece 13 and not any underlying fabric.

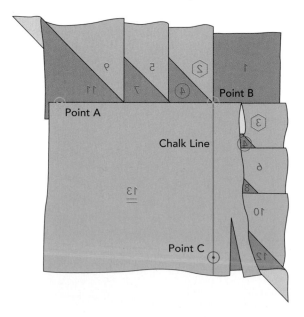

Trim seam allowance to ¼".

e. Turn back piece 13, exposing its wrong side.

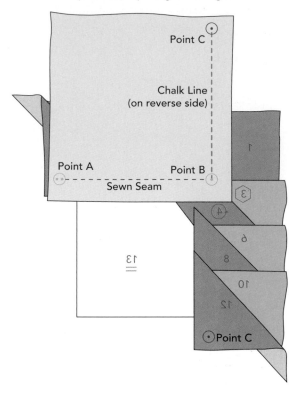

Turn back piece 13.

f. Press the seam allowance along the marked chalk line. Trim one layer of the seam allowance at an angle to reduce bulk.

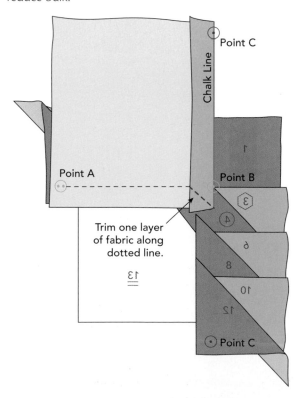

Press seam allowance along chalk line.

g. Fold the corner of the seam allowance at Point B diagonally and press. Include as much of the seam allowance as possible.

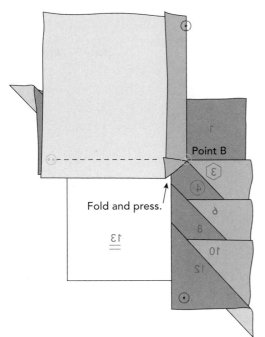

Fold corner of seam allowance diagonally and press.

h. Complete the second leg of piece 13 by hand sewing, using the blind-hem (or zigzag) stitch, or fusing (pages 17–18). Whichever option you choose, flip-flop piece 13 will be pressed and then secured into its final position, and this block is history.

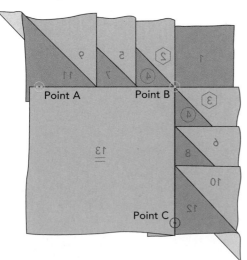

Press second leg of piece 13 into place, then sew or fuse.

By this point some of my directions may be sounding oddly familiar. To avoid inducing an alarming sense of déjà vu, the directions in the next chapters will be abbreviated, detailing only that which is new and allowing you to refer back to Chapters 2–5 for specifics if you need to refresh your memory.

PRACTICE YOUR SKILLS: DELECTABLE MOUNTAIN

Before moving on to the next chapter, you may want to try the Delectable Mountain block. It looks quite similar to the Sawtooth; however, because the peaks or toes point in a different direction, a smooth, raw-edge-free surface will not be created at Point B. As a result, before the first leg of flip-flop piece 16 is sewn, the seam allowance sticking in its way must be pinned aside. Remember, "When seams collide, pin one aside." (See page 28 for a review of this procedure.)

In addition, as you foundation piece the triangles of this block, note that pieces 14 and 15 are positioned in a different direction than all the others.

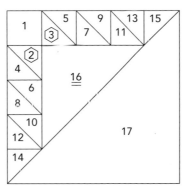
Foundation with Instructions

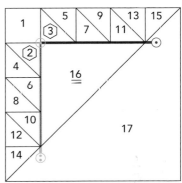
Highlighted Instructional Block

Point A = ⊙⊙
Point B = ⊙
Point C = ⊙

Completed Block: Delectable Mountain

Sawtooth

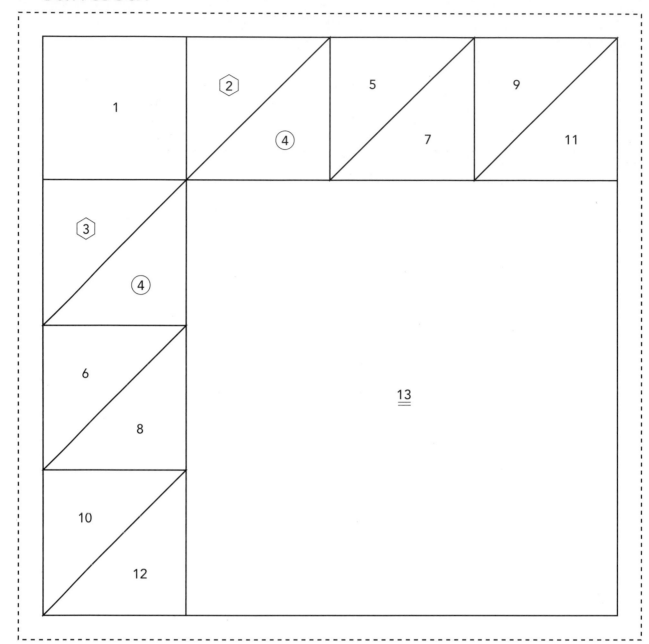

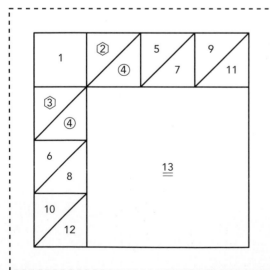

Delectable Mountain

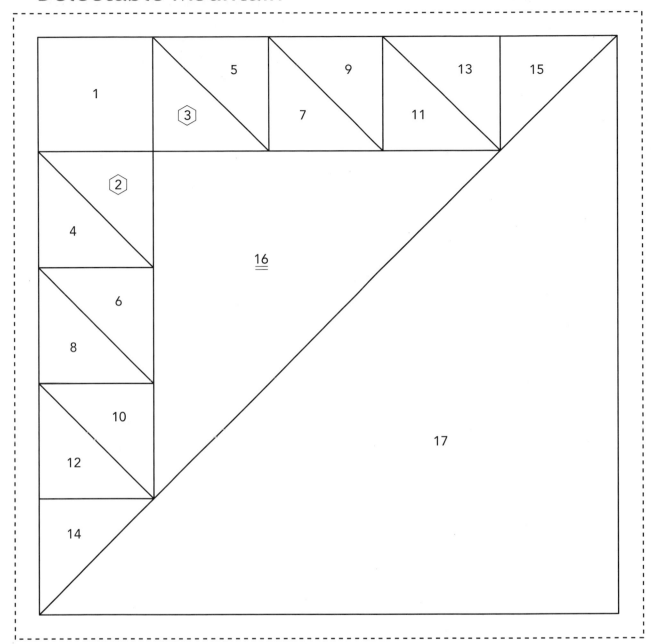

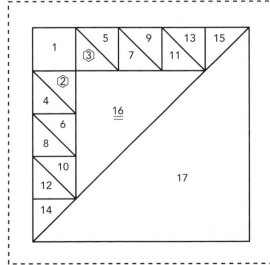

6 Ring Around the Circle with Partial Seam Piecing
(Big O and Twist)

INTRODUCTION

Partial seam piecing is ideally suited for a flip-flop type of assembly. The Big O block is partial seam piecing at its most basic. In previous chapters, the portion of the block to be completed on the unprinted Fabric Side was always part of a newly added, separate flip-flop piece. In flip-flop-style partial seam piecing, the portion of the block to be completed is only the remainder of a seamline already partially sewn. The unsewn remainder will be the flip-flopped "mock" seam that is fused (or sewn) into place from the unprinted Fabric Side of the foundation.

On the Foundation with Instructions, the symbol for partial seam piecing is the presence of two numbers on a single piece with arrows indicating portions of the seam to be sewn in each step. Point B indicates where to stop the first part of the partial seam and where to start the second part of that same seam later in the block's construction when it's flip-flop time.

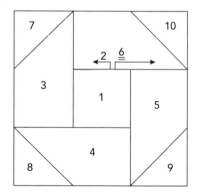

Foundation with Instructions

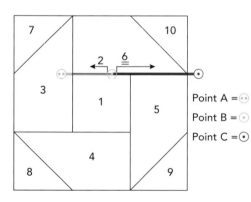

Highlighted Instructional Block

Point A = ⊙⊙
Point B = ⊙
Point C = ⊙

Completed Block: Big O

BIG O BLOCK CONSTRUCTION

Unless otherwise specified, your stitched seamline should be ¼" longer than the printed line at each side, extending into an adjacent piece at each end.

1. Place piece 1 right side up on the unprinted Fabric Side. Place piece 2/6 right side down on top of piece 1.

2. On the Printed Side, sew the first leg, starting at Point A and stopping at Point B. This is the partial seam part of partial seam piecing.

3. Insert pins at Points B and C to mark the seamline for the second leg. Go straight up from the Printed side, where Points B and C are clearly visible, through to the unprinted Fabric Side.

4. Place a thin, see-through ruler over piece 2/6, from Point B through Point C, using the pins as your guideline. Draw a line from Point B through Point C to mark the seamline for the second leg. Be sure to use a marker that is washable and incapable of being heat set by an iron. Remove the pins.

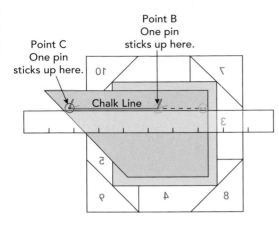

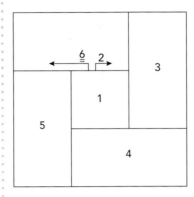

Draw seamline from Point B through Point C.

5. Fold along the marked chalk line and press into place. The folded seamline is the unsewn portion of the partial seam. It will be sewn (or fused) later, *not* now.

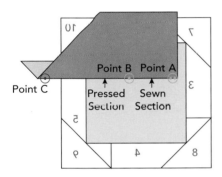

Press piece 2/6 into place.

6. Sew pieces 3 and 4 as you would in traditional foundation piecing (pages 9–10).

7. Pin piece 2/6 out of the way.

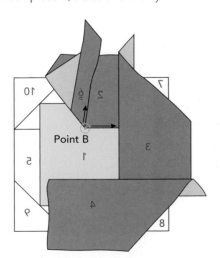

Pin piece 2/6 out of the way.

8. Sew piece 5 as you would in traditional foundation piecing.

9. Unpin piece 2/6. Press it back into place. Complete the second leg from the Fabric Side by hand sewing, using the machine blind-hem (or zigzag) stitch, or fusing (pages 17–18).

10. Sew pieces 7–10 just as you would in traditional foundation piecing.

PRACTICE YOUR SKILLS: TWIST

Another basic block using partial seam piecing is this little gem, aptly named Twist.

Foundation with Instructions   Highlighted Instructional Block

Point A = ⊙⊙
Point B = ⊙
Point C = ⊙

Completed Block: Twist

Big O

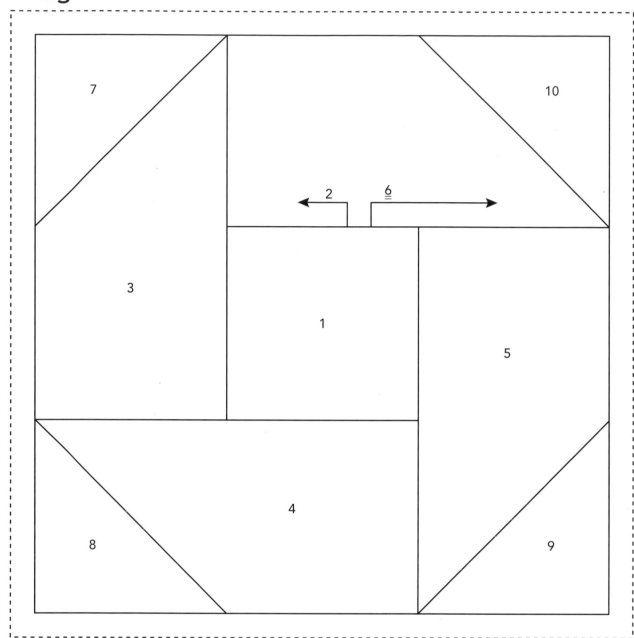

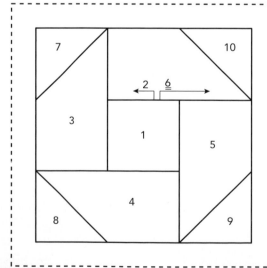

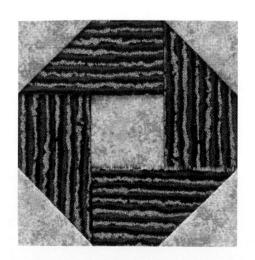

Twist

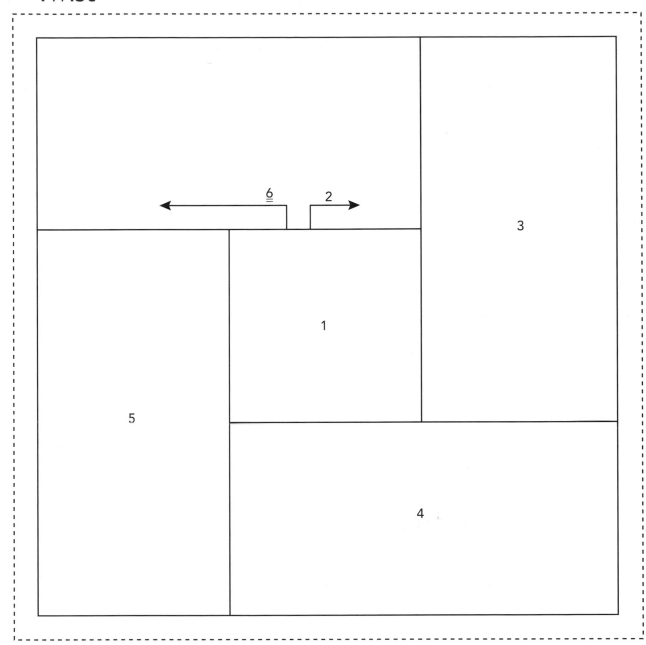

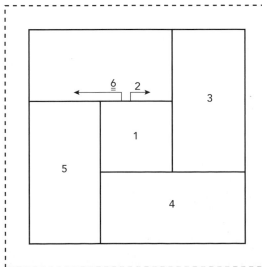

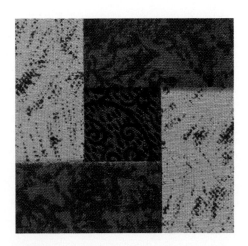

KEEP GOING

7 Two Become One

(King's X and Maltese Cross)

INTRODUCTION

To flip-flop your way through hundreds of additional blocks, you can temporarily slice the paper foundation in half, producing two parts that will very soon be reunited into one.

The slice line drawn to separate the two halves of the block always divides the foundation into two equal parts. This line follows a seamline through the center section and continues right through one or more pieces to the edge of the block. Don't worry. The foundation will be a single piece again before the fabric to cover these divided pieces is added.

Examples of classic blocks that benefit from this Two Become One construction are the LeMoyne Star, the Cowboy's Star, and the Arkansas Traveler, not to mention King's X featured here.

The only new symbol to learn in this chapter is the Slice Line. Before any sewing is begun, the paper foundation will be cut apart along that line. The foundation will then be taped back together once the two halves are reunited as the completed 1–4 unit is sewn to the completed 5–8 unit.

KING'S X BLOCK CONSTRUCTION

Unless otherwise specified, your stitched seamline should be ¼" longer than the printed line at each side, extending into an adjacent piece at each end.

1. Slice the paper foundation into two sections along the slice line.

2. Sew pieces 1–4 on the first half of the foundation, placing fabric on the unprinted Fabric Side and sewing on the Printed Side. Extend the seams at both ends on all pieces.

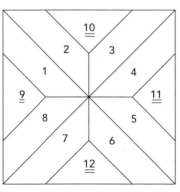

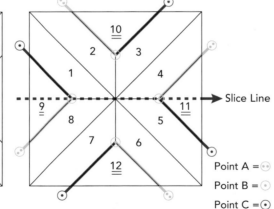

Point A = ⊙⊙
Point B = ⊙
Point C = ⊙

Foundation with Instructions   Highlighted Instructional Block

Completed Block: King's X

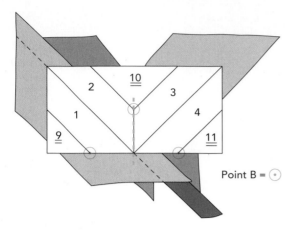

Point B = ⊙

Sew extended seam between pieces 2 and 3.
Press piece 3 into place.

> **NOTE:** The extension of the seamline between pieces 2 and 3 is particularly important. That seam starts at the far edge of the bottom seam allowance and runs straight up the center of the block and ¼″ into the space of the adjacent piece 10. Extending the seamline at the lower end will help create a flat seam allowance. The extension at the upper end is essential for preparing a smooth surface that is ready to receive flip-flop piece 10.

3. Sew pieces 5–8 on the second half of the foundation, exactly as you did pieces 1–4 on the first (Step 2). Extend the seams at both ends on all pieces.

4. To sew the two halves of the foundation back together, place the halves with Fabric Sides together. Sew along the Slice Line, catching only the fabric and not the paper foundation. Extend the seamlines at both ends, sewing a generous ¼″ past each Point B. For added stability, place a piece of notebook paper under the two foundations as you sew this seamline. Tear the notebook paper away once the seam is sewn.

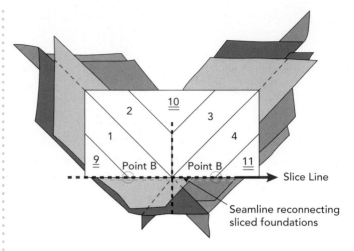

Place foundation halves Fabric Sides together and sew.

5. Trim the seam allowance to ¼″. Press open the seam and tape the unsewn portions of the paper foundation back together.

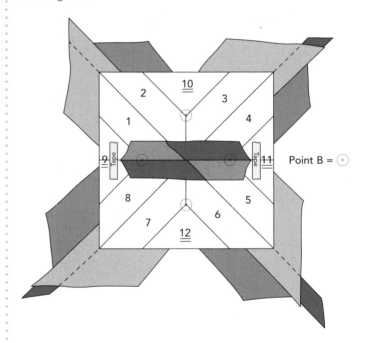

Point B = ⊙

Trim and press seam allowance open.
Tape foundations back together.

6. Sew flip-flop pieces 9–12. Sew the green leg first from the Printed Side, then sew or fuse the red leg from the unprinted Fabric Side (page 17). Because you extended the seams between pieces 2 and 3, 4 and 5, and so on, you have a smooth surface for these flip-flop pieces. No seam allowances need to be pinned out of the way.

PRACTICE YOUR SKILLS: MALTESE CROSS

To practice the extremely useful Two Become One maneuver, try the following block, known as the Maltese or King's Cross.

Remember to cut along the Slice Line first. Then sew pieces 1–4 on the first section and 5–8 on the other. Next sew the two sections together along the Slice Line where possible. Use tape to finish the reunion where necessary. After that, it is just traditional foundation piecing all the way home.

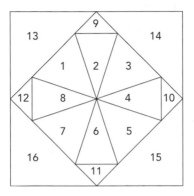

Foundation with Instructions

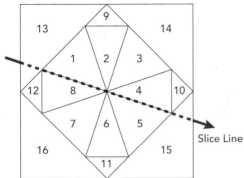

Highlighted Instructional Block

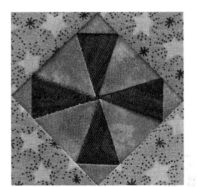

Completed Block: Maltese Cross

King's X

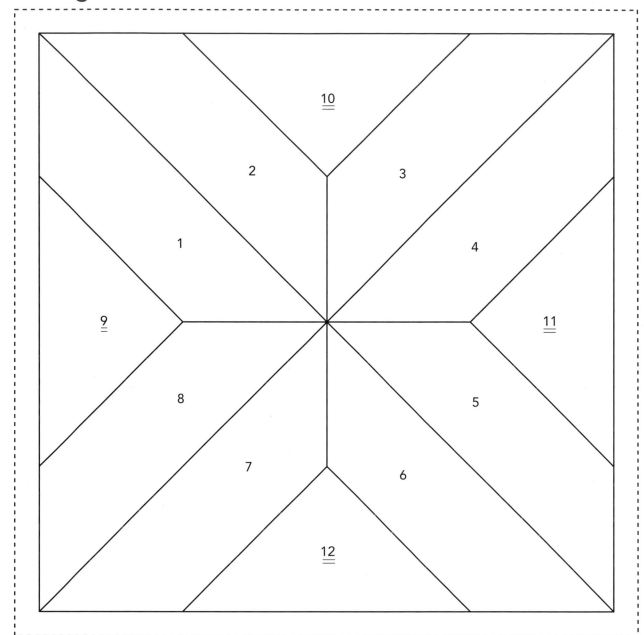

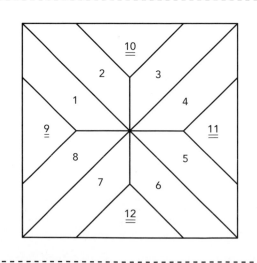

King's X

Maltese Cross

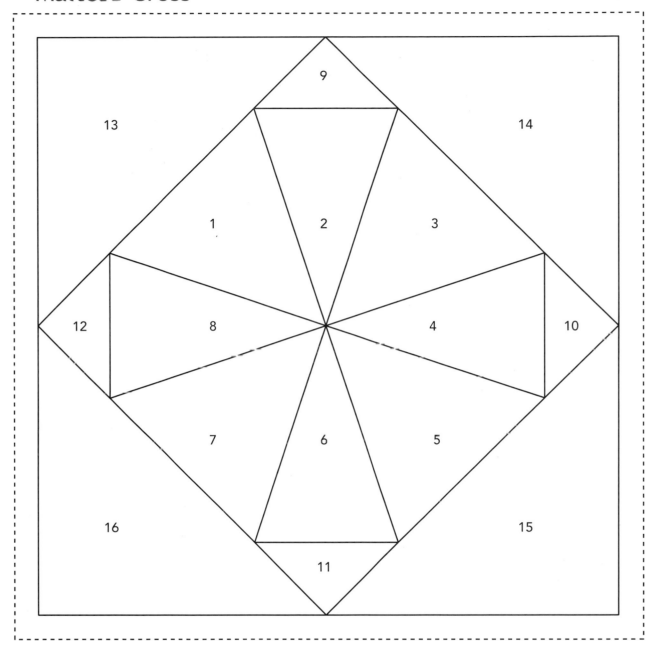

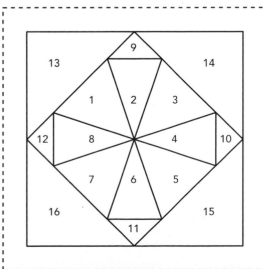

8 Demystifying the Green Leg Versus Red Leg
(Hidden Star and Star in a Star in a Star)

INTRODUCTION

The selection of the green leg versus red leg—that is, which of the legs of a flip-flop piece goes first and which goes second—is not random. There is a method that determines the best choice. The decision made will affect the quality of the block, as well as the ease with which its seams are sewn. For more detailed information on how to choose which leg is which, see the Appendix (page 93).

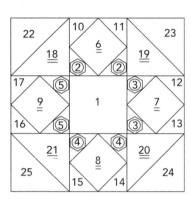

Foundation with Instructions

Highlighted Instructional Block

Point A = ⊙⊙
Point B = ⊙
Point C = ⊙

Completed Block: Hidden Star

HIDDEN STAR BLOCK CONSTRUCTION

Note that because flip-flop pieces 6–9 can be completed with either leg first, no green or red highlighting is given for these pieces in the Highlighted Instructional Block.

Unless otherwise specified, your stitched seamline should be ¼" longer than the printed line at each side, extending into an adjacent piece at each end.

1. Place piece 1 right side up on the unprinted Fabric Side of the foundation.

2. Cut a piece of fabric large enough to cover both pieces 2 and 2 and the space between them. Place this single, large piece of fabric right side down on the unprinted Fabric Side. Sew on the Printed Side. Sew pieces 2 and 2 as one, starting and stopping precisely at each Point B.

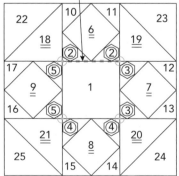

Piece 2 sewn dot to dot

Point B = ⊙

PRINTED SIDE
Sew piece 2 dot to dot.

3. Press and pin piece 2 out of the way before you add piece 3.

4. Cut and sew pieces 3 and 3, 4 and 4, and 5 and 5 exactly as you did pieces 2 and 2 (Steps 2–3).

5. Sew flip-flop piece 6. Sew the first leg from the Printed Side. Because the surface provided by the large piece 2 and 2 is smooth, either leg of piece 6 could be chosen as the first/green leg.

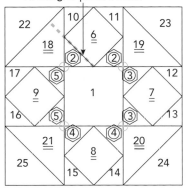

First leg of piece 6 sewn

PRINTED SIDE
Sew first leg of piece 6.

6. Sew or fuse the second leg of piece 6 from the unprinted Fabric Side (pages 17–18).

7. Sew flip-flop pieces 7–9 exactly as you sewed piece 6 (Steps 5–6).

8. Sew pieces 10–17 as you would in traditional foundation piecing (pages 9–10).

9. Sew the first leg of flip-flop piece 18 from the Printed Side, first pinning the protruding seam allowance of piece 5 out of the way, stopping exactly at Point B. Remove the pin. Press the seam allowance of piece 5 back into place.

10. Sew or fuse the second leg of piece 18 from the unprinted Fabric Side (pages 17–18).

11. Sew flip-flop pieces 19–21 exactly as you sewed piece 18 (Steps 9–10).

12. Sew pieces 22–25 as you would in traditional foundation piecing (pages 9–10).

PRACTICE YOUR SKILLS:
STAR IN A STAR IN A STAR

The following Star in a Star in a Star block provides practice and practice and more practice in selecting the green and red legs. This block is also a good illustration of just how easy it is to work with miniature pieces using Flip-Flop Paper Piecing.

Note that because flip-flop pieces 6–9, 18–21, and 30–33 can be completed with either leg first, no green or red highlighting is given for these pieces on the Highlighted Instructional Block. Refer to the 6″ pattern on page 55 for the center numbers and symbols for the blocks below and for the 2¼″ pattern, also on page 55.

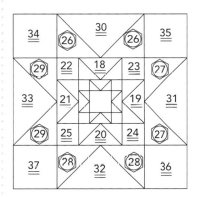

Foundation with Instructions   Highlighted Instructional Block

Point A = ⊙⊙
Point B = ⊙
Point C = ⊙

Completed Block: Star in a Star in a Star

Hidden Star

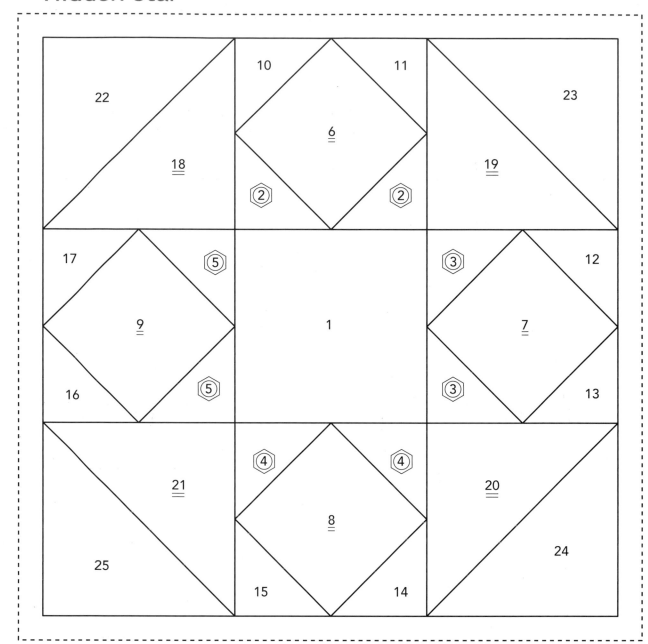

22 / <u>18</u>	10 / 11 / <u>6</u> / ②②	23 / <u>19</u>
17 / ⑤ / <u>9</u> / ⑤ / 16	1	③ / 12 / <u>7</u> / ③ / 13
<u>21</u> / 25	④④ / <u>8</u> / 15 / 14	<u>20</u> / 24

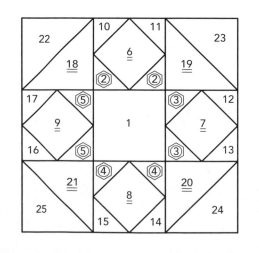

Star in a Star in a Star

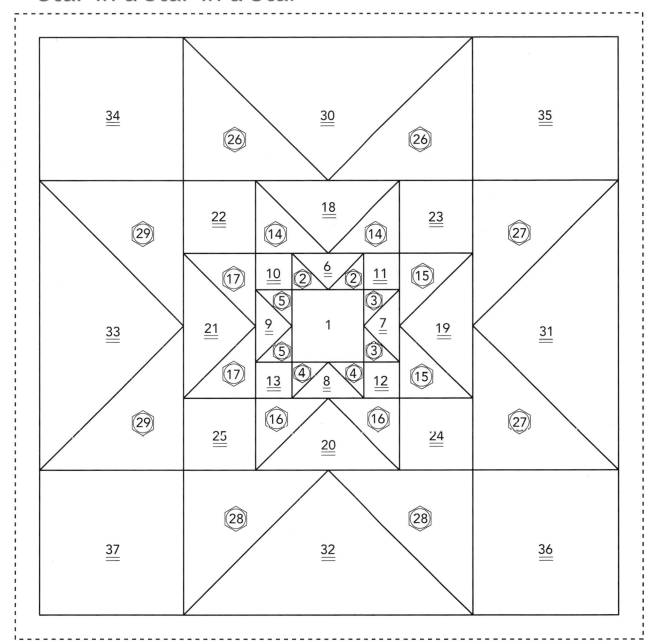

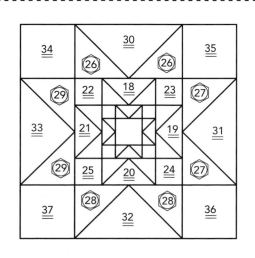

CHAPTER:

9 Strip Flips

(Cheyenne and Arrowhead)

INTRODUCTION

Throughout the previous eight chapters, you may have been suffering from rotary-cutting withdrawal. Well, get out that cutter and mat, because it is time to do some strip piecing. If you are hopelessly old-fashioned (like me), just use scissors. Whichever your choice of cutting tool, you will sew two fabrics into strip sets to make a Strip Flip type of block.

This technique, like many before, opens up a whole new array of blocks that can be constructed on a single foundation, flip-flop style.

The new symbol to be learned in this block is the "s" (for strip) written after a number that overlaps two pieces. These pieces are constructed from a single strip set prepared before you do any sewing on the foundation. Point D on the foundation marks the point where you will pin the seam of the strip set.

CHEYENNE BLOCK CONSTRUCTION

Unless otherwise specified, your stitched seamline should be ¼" longer than the printed line at each side, extending into an adjacent piece at each end.

1. For pieces 6s–9s, cut 1 strip from each of 2 fabrics (3" × 12" for the 6" block and 1½" × 7" for the 2¼" block). Sew the strips together. Press open the seam allowance.

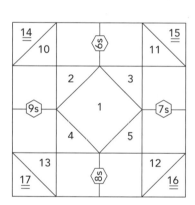

Foundation with Instructions

Highlighted Instructional Block

Point A = ⊙⊙
Point B = ⊙
Point C = ⊙
Point D = ⊙

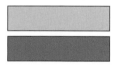

Cut 2 strips.

Sew 2 strips using ¼" seam allowance. Press.

2. Subcut the strip set into 4 equal pieces

Completed Block: Cheyenne

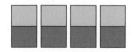

Subcut.

3. Sew pieces 1–5 as you would in traditional foundation piecing (pages 9–10).

4. Insert a pin at Point D, going straight up from the Printed Side to the unprinted Fabric Side. Place 6s right side down on the Fabric Side, using the pin as a guide. The center seam of piece 6s will exactly match the seamline at Point D. Pin 6s in place.

5. On the Printed Side, sew piece 6s from Point B to Point B. Sew precisely from dot to dot to avoid a head-on collision with pieces 10 and 11, which will be added later.

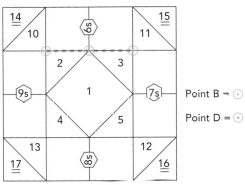

Match center seam of strip set 6s with Point D.

6. Press piece 6s into place, lining up the center seamline with the line on the paper foundation. Pin the piece to the paper foundation. In addition to properly aligning piece 6s, this step will also ensure that piece 6s is not in the way when you add piece 7s.

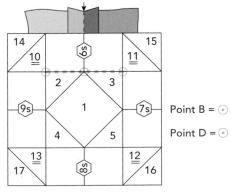

Press and pin piece 6s into place.

7. Sew pieces 7s–9s exactly as you sewed piece 6s (Steps 4–5).

8. Sew flip-flop pieces 10–13. Sew the green leg first from the Printed Side, then sew or fuse the red leg from the unprinted Fabric Side (pages 17–18).

9. Sew pieces 14–17 as you would in traditional foundation piecing (pages 9–10).

PRACTICE YOUR SKILLS: ARROWHEAD

To make the Arrowhead block, piece a dark strip and a light strip: Cut 2" × 21" for the 6" block and 1" × 9" for the 2¼" block. In a block such as this one, in which one strip set (3s) is shorter than the others (4s–7s), don't subcut the strip set into pieces before beginning to construct the block. Instead, use the entire strip set as needed and trim it off after each use.

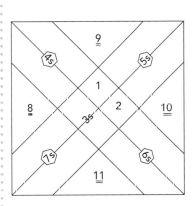

| Foundation with Instructions | Highlighted Instructional Block |

Point A = ⊙
Point B = ⊙
Point C = ⊙
Point D = ⊙

Completed Block: Arrowhead

Cheyenne

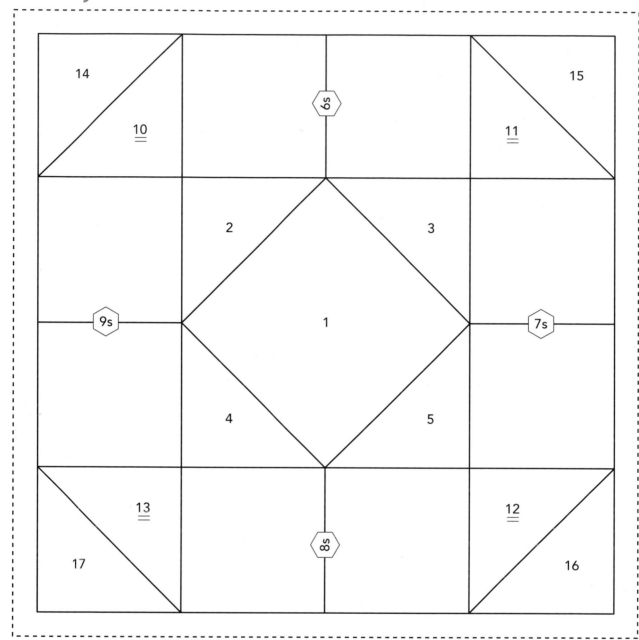

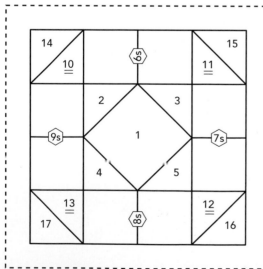

Arrowhead

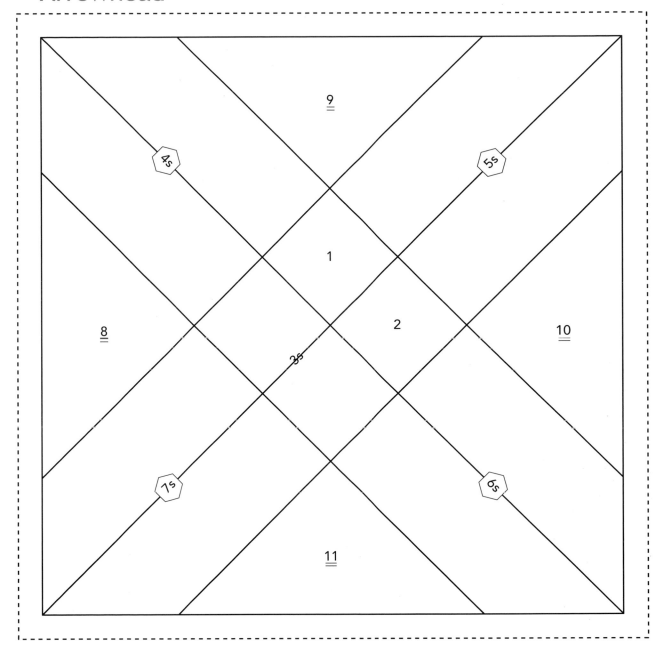

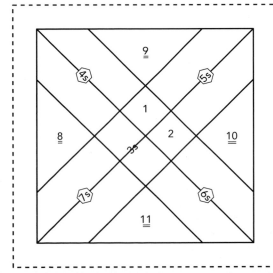

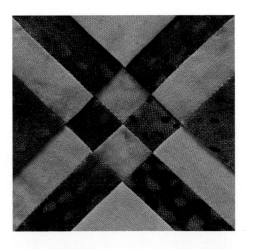

10 Invisible Strip Flips

(Ohio Star with Star Tip Color Variations and Evening Star with Alternating Star Tip Fabrics)

INTRODUCTION

Just as in the regular Strip Flips of Chapter 9, Invisible Strip Flips are produced by joining two fabrics to form strip sets. The difference is that after the final construction of the Invisible Strip Flip block, the seam that joins the two fabrics will be "invisible." The function of this magic trick is to avoid a collision of seam allowances and to provide a nice, smooth surface for flip-flop pieces that will be added right on top of the strip sets. Please read on. I assure you that these words of mystery will soon become abundantly clear.

The symbol used for Invisible Strip Flips is a repeat of that used for regular Strip Flips—an "s" (for strip) added after the piece number. However, with Invisible Strip Flips, you will see each number twice. In reality 6s and 6s will be one single strip set piece when sewn onto the block. Please read on and all will be clear.

OHIO STAR WITH STAR TIP COLOR VARIATIONS BLOCK CONSTRUCTION

Unless otherwise specified, your stitched seamline should be ¼" longer than the printed line at each side, extending into an adjacent piece at each end.

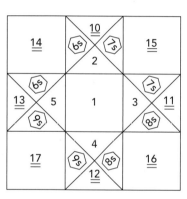

Foundation with Instructions

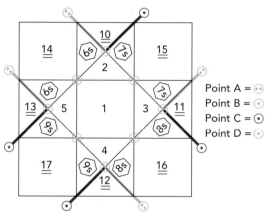

Point A = ⊙⊙
Point B = ⊙
Point C = ⊙
Point D = ⊙

Highlighted Instructional Block

1. For pieces 6s–9s, cut 1 strip from each of 2 fabrics (2½" × 16" for the 6" block and 1¼" × 6" for the 2¼" block). Sew the strips together. Press open the seam allowance.

Cut 2 strips.

Sew 2 strips using ¼" seam allowance. Press.

2. Subcut the strip set into 4 equal pieces.

Subcut strip set.

Completed Block: Ohio Star with Star Tip Color Variations

3. Sew pieces 1–5 as you would in traditional foundation piecing (pages 9–10).

4. Insert a pin at Point D, going straight up from the Printed Side to the Fabric Side. Place 6s right side down on the Fabric Side, using the pin as a guide. The center seam of piece 6s will exactly match Point D. Pin 6s in place.

5. Sew piece 6s from Point B to Point B, precisely dot to dot. Press into position both sides of 6s, each of which will form a star tip later. Pin 6s to foundation.

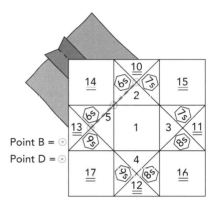

Point B = ⊙
Point D = ⊙

Sew piece 6s, press, and pin.

6. Sew pieces 7s–9s exactly as you sewed piece 6s (Steps 4–5).

7. Sew flip-flop pieces 10–13. Sew the green leg first from the Printed Side, then sew or fuse the red leg from the unprinted Fabric Side (pages 17–18).

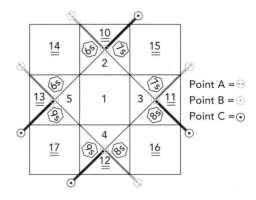

Point A = ⊚
Point B = ⊙
Point C = ⊙

Sew green leg first, then red leg.

8. Sew flip-flop pieces 14–17. Sew the green leg first from the Printed Side, stopping the stitching at Point D. Sew or fuse the red leg from the unprinted Fabric Side (pages 17–18).

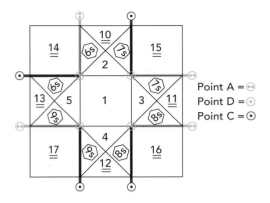

Point A = ⊚
Point D = ⊙
Point C = ⊙

Sew green leg first, then red leg.

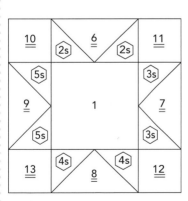 **NOTE:** As you sew these flip-flop pieces, the center seams on the strip sets will be hidden and become invisible. Magic!

PRACTICE YOUR SKILLS: EVENING STAR WITH ALTERNATING STAR TIP FABRICS

Evening Star with Alternating Star Tip Fabrics can be sewn using a strip set prepared for pieces 2s through 5s. Cut two strips (2¾" × 14" for a 6" block and 1¼" × 6" for a 2¼" block). Sew the pieces together with a ¼" seam and press open.

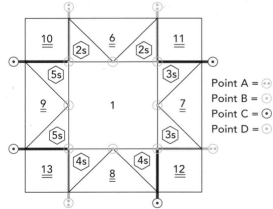

Point A = ⊚
Point B = ⊙
Point C = ⊙
Point D = ⊙

Foundation with Instructions   Highlighted Instructional Block

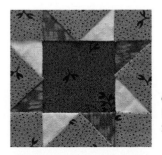

Completed Block:
Evening Star with Alternating
Star Tip Fabrics

Ohio Star

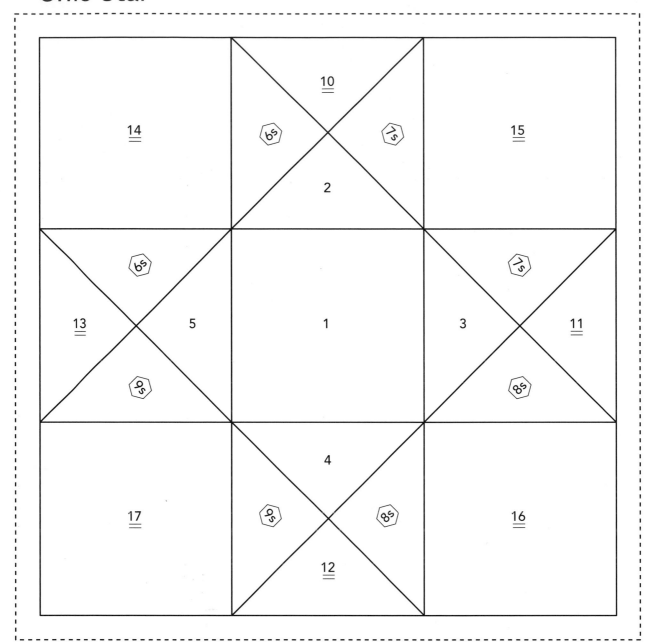

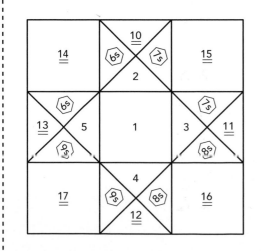

Evening Star

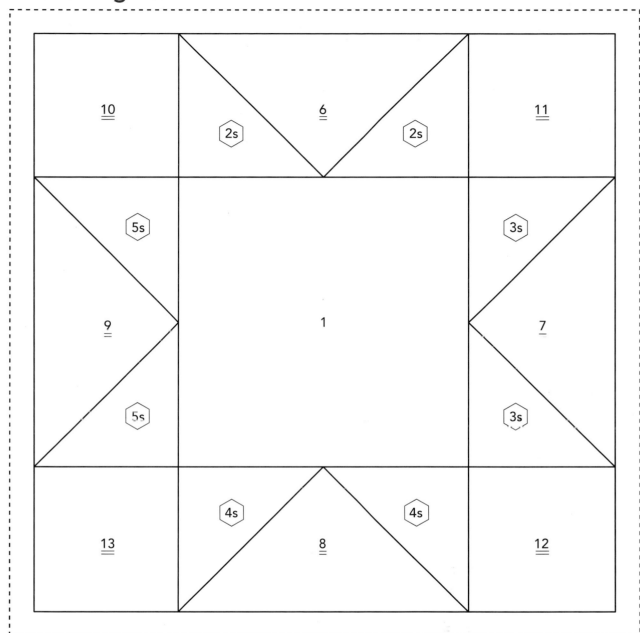

10	6 (2s) (2s)	11
5s		3s
9	1	7
5s		3s
13	4s 8 4s	12

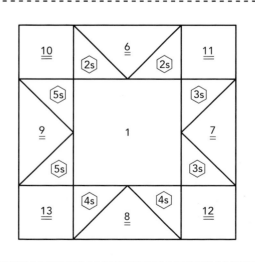

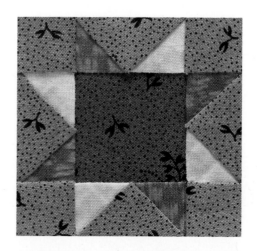

Evening Star

Flip-Flop Appliqué
(Four-Basket Block and Necktie)

INTRODUCTION

A tisket, a tasket, a little flip-flop basket. Bad poetry maybe, but nothing is sweeter on a springtime quilt than a Basket block. I am especially fond of quilts with dozens of miniature baskets. No technique is better for basket building en masse than Flip-Flop Paper Piecing. In fact, the example in this chapter will yield four baskets to the block. Thus, a simple 20-block quilt would produce 80 baskets, whereas a 30-block quilt would overwhelm any Easter bunny. This all goes to show that a bit of appliqué *can* be added as you progress through a flip-flop block.

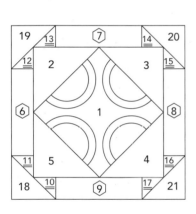

Foundation with Instructions

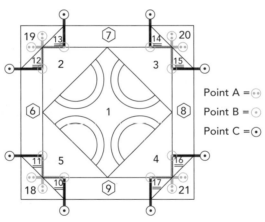

Highlighted Instructional Block

Point A = ⊙⊙
Point B = ⊙
Point C = ⊙

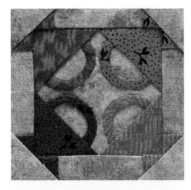

Completed Block: Four-Basket Block

This block introduces the concept of combining simple appliqué with piecing. In this example, a set of handles is sewn to piece 1 before adding pieces 2–5, which cover the raw ends. Consider using cording for the handles of the 2¼" block. Of course, Easter eggs, fruit, flowers, or whatever could also be spilling out of each basket.

FOUR-BASKET BLOCK CONSTRUCTION

Unless otherwise specified, your stitched seamline should be ¼" longer than the printed line at each side, extending into an adjacent piece at each end.

1. Copy the paper foundation, making sure to include the handle lines for placement.

2. Cut bias strips for the fabric handles—one for each basket (1" × 3½" for the 6" block and ⅝" × 1¾" for the 2¼" block). Fold each strip in half lengthwise.

Cut bias strips.

Fold in half.

3. Place piece 1 right side up on the unprinted Fabric Side of the foundation and pin in place.

4. Trace the handle placement lines on the fabric. Use chalk or a washable marker that is incapable of being heat set. Hold up the block to a window or lightbox, if necessary, when tracing.

5. Place the raw edges of a fabric handle next to the outer line of a traced handle. Pin in place. Be sure the ends of the fabric handles extend into the next piece (2, 3, 4, or 5) so these pieces will cover the raw ends of the handles.

Match raw edge of handle to curve of outer handle line.

6. Sew on the inner traced line of the handle on the unprinted Fabric Side. Make sure the stitching extends into the adjacent piece (2, 3, 4, or 5) at both ends.

Sew handle in place.

7. Trim the raw edges of the handle piece to an ⅛" seam allowance.

8. Press the handle up over the raw edges to follow the outer traced line. Sew in place using invisible (monofilament) thread with a blind-hem, zigzag, or hand stitch.

Press handle over raw edges, then stitch.

9. Sew the other 3 handles in the same manner as the first.

10. Sew pieces 2–5 as you would in traditional foundation piecing (pages 9–10). Note that the raw edges of the handles are now covered and sewn into a seam allowance.

11. Sew pieces 6–9, starting and stopping precisely at each Point B.

12. Sew flip-flop pieces 10–17. Sew the green leg from the Printed Side, then sew or fuse the red leg from the unprinted Fabric Side (pages 17–18).

13. Sew pieces 18–21 as you would in traditional foundation piecing (pages 9–10).

Four miniature baskets with matching handles! Flip-flopping is absolutely the best technique for basket construction. The use of a single foundation ensures uniformity in size, despite the multiple pieces involved.

PRACTICE YOUR SKILLS: NECKTIE

You can add appliqué at many steps along the way, from beginning to end.
An appliqué may even be the final piece itself. Just check out this great Necktie
variation, in which a circle is appliquéd after all other pieces are in place. Note
that piece 4 is sewn flip-flop style—first the green leg, then the red leg.

Foundation with Instructions

Highlighted Instructional Block

Point A = ⊙⊙
Point B = ⊙
Point C = ⊙

Completed Block: Necktie

Four-Basket Block

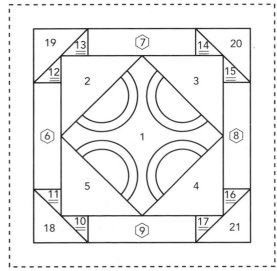

Four-Basket Block

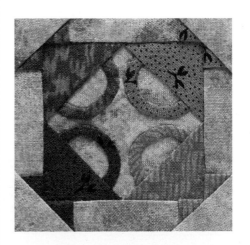

Necktie

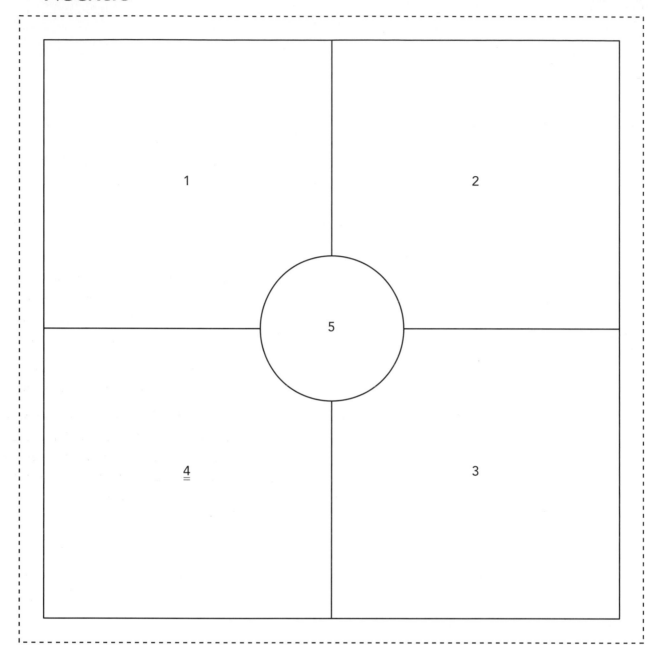

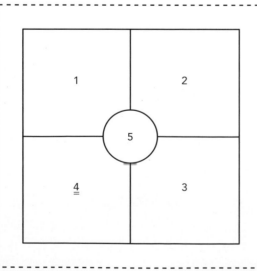

12 From Outside In

(Crosspatch and Calico Spools)

INTRODUCTION

This chapter contains one of the simplest blocks in the book, but it illustrates one of the most useful concepts: A block need not be constructed by starting at the center and going out (like Birds in the Air) or even by starting at one corner and progressing to the others (like Sawtooth). Instead a block can be constructed from the outside in—that is, starting from two outside edges and working toward the center. Indeed, it is even possible to start at four outside corners and then go inward, but two will do for now.

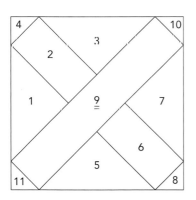

Foundation with Instructions

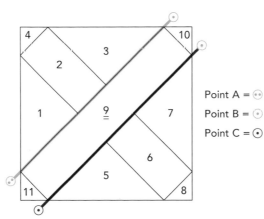

Point A = ⊙⊙
Point B = ⊙
Point C = ⊙

Highlighted Instructional Block

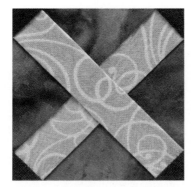

Completed Block: Crosspatch

CROSSPATCH BLOCK CONSTRUCTION

Unless otherwise specified, your stitched seamline should be ¼" longer than the printed line at each side, extending into an adjacent piece at each end.

1. Sew pieces 1–8 as you would in traditional foundation piecing (pages 9–10).

2. Place flip-flop piece 9 right side down on the unprinted Fabric Side. Make sure it covers the green leg; touches pieces 1, 2, and 3; and extends into the seam allowance at the edges of the block.

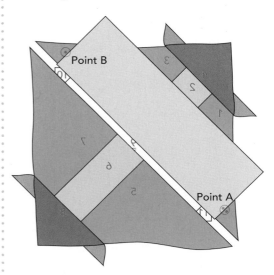

Place piece 9 right side down on Fabric Side.

3. Sew the green leg first from the Printed Side.

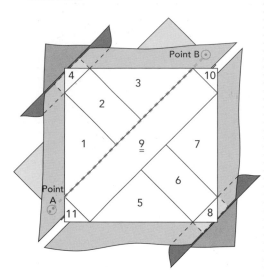

Sew green leg of piece 9 from Printed Side

4. Sew or fuse the red leg from the unprinted Fabric Side (page 17).

5. Sew pieces 10 and 11 as you would in traditional foundation piecing (page 9).

CAUTION

This technique is wonderfully versatile, but a word of warning to those of you who, like me, are enchanted by miniature quilts. In drafting a block with the From Outside In type of construction, do *not* make the center flip-flop piece any narrower than ¼". Sadly, I speak from experience.

PRACTICE YOUR SKILLS: CALICO SPOOLS

The Outside In maneuver is the key to completing this block, which is historically named Calico Spools. To me, it looks more like a butterfly than a spool, calico or otherwise.

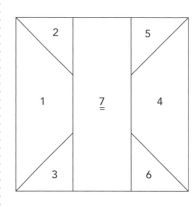

Foundation with Instructions   Highlighted Instructional Block

Point A = ⊙⊙
Point B = ⊙
Point C = ⊙

Completed Block: Calico Spools

Crosspatch

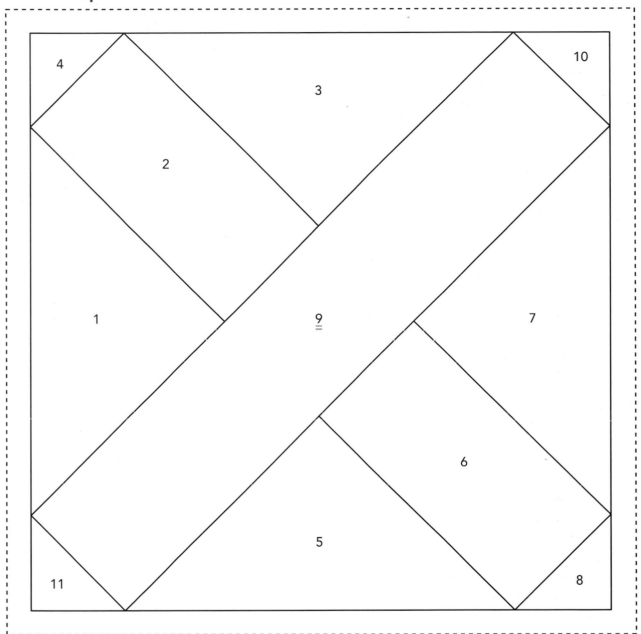

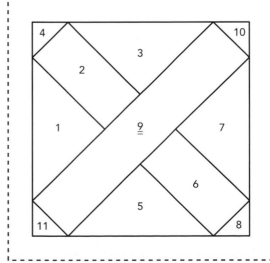

Calico Spools

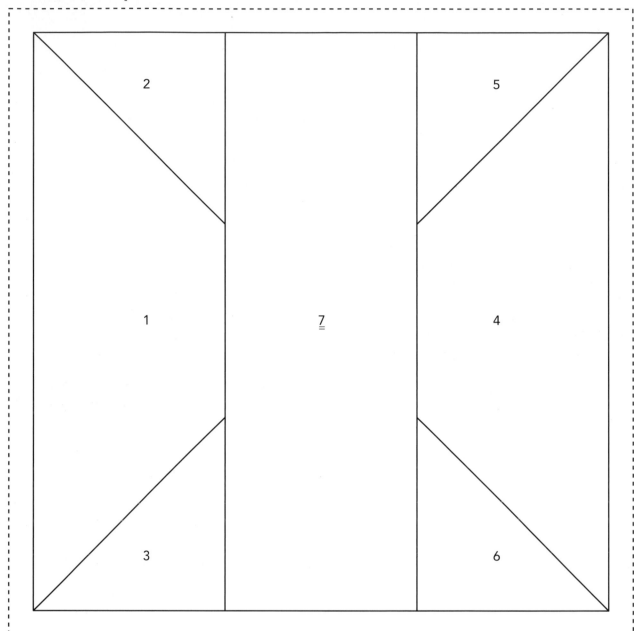

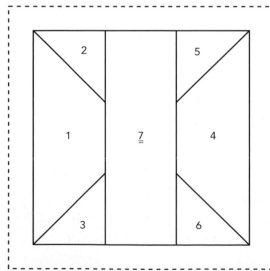

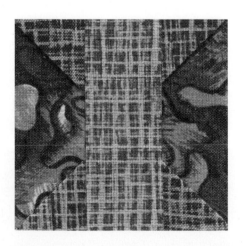

13 Pete and Repeat

(Mrs. Cleveland's Choice and Garden of Eden)

INTRODUCTION

Many blocks that appear to be complicated are actually quite simple. It is often possible to use a single technique described in one of the preceding chapters and just repeat and repeat and repeat it throughout the block. The effect is magnificent. The work is basic flip-flopping.

One example is Mrs. Cleveland's Choice. The entire block—all 65 pieces—can be sewn on a single paper foundation, using the most basic of maneuvers: the simple flip-flop used for Birds in the Air. Review Chapter 2 (pages 14–19) if you need more information than is given here.

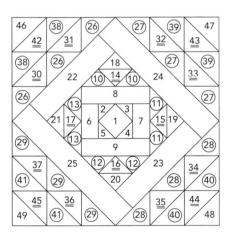

Foundation with Instructions

Completed Block: Mrs. Cleveland's Choice

Note that no Highlighted Instructional Block is provided: All flip-flop pieces can be completed with either leg first.

MRS. CLEVELAND'S CHOICE BLOCK CONSTRUCTION

Unless otherwise specified, your stitched seamline should be ¼" longer than the printed line at each side, extending into an adjacent piece at each end.

1. Sew pieces 1–9 as you would in traditional foundation piecing (pages 9–10).

2. Cut a single piece of fabric large enough to cover both pieces 10 and 10 and the space between them.

3. Sew pieces 10 and 10 as you would in traditional foundation piecing (pages 9–10). The only difference is that the fabric will cover more than one piece at a time.

4. Cut and sew pieces 11 and 11, 12 and 12, and 13 and 13 exactly as you sewed pieces 10 and 10 (Steps 2–3).

5. Sew flip-flop pieces 14–17. Sew the first leg from the Printed Side, then sew or fuse the second leg from the unprinted Fabric Side (pages 17–18).

6. Sew pieces 18–25 as you would in traditional foundation piecing.

7. Cut a single piece of fabric large enough to cover pieces 26, 26, and 26 and the spaces between them.

8. Sew pieces 26, 26, and 26 as you would in traditional foundation piecing. The only difference is that the fabric will cover more than one piece at a time.

9. Cut and sew pieces 27–29 exactly as you sewed piece 26 (Steps 7–8).

10. Sew flip-flop pieces 30–37. Sew the first leg from the Printed Side, then sew or fuse the second leg from the unprinted Fabric Side (pages 17–18).

11. Cut a single piece of fabric large enough to cover pieces 38 and 38 and the spaces between them.

12. Sew pieces 38 and 38 as you would in traditional foundation piecing.

13. Cut and sew piece 39 and 39, 40 and 40, and 41 and 41 exactly as you sewed pieces 38 and 38 (Steps 11–12).

14. Sew flip-flop pieces 42–45. Sew the first leg from the Printed Side, then sew or fuse the second leg from the unprinted Fabric Side (pages 17–18).

15. Sew pieces 46–49 as you would in traditional foundation piecing.

16. Take your completed block to your next guild or bee meeting. At Show and Tell, show them that you've made Mrs. Cleveland proud. Then tell them that you did it all on a single piece of paper.

PRACTICE YOUR SKILLS: GARDEN OF EDEN

The Garden of Eden block illustrates a triple Pete and Repeat of the From Outside In maneuver (Chapter 12). As in Mrs. Cleveland's Choice, no Highlighted Instructional Block is needed because all flip-flop pieces (21–23) can be sewn with either leg first.

The Garden of Eden is a particularly useful block because so many traditional blocks have a similar structure: crossed sashing strips running straight through the middle of a block.

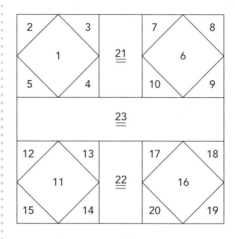

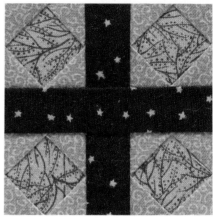

Foundation with Instructions   Completed Block: Garden of Eden

Mrs. Cleveland's Choice

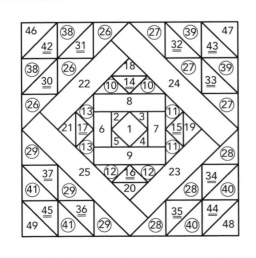

Garden of Eden

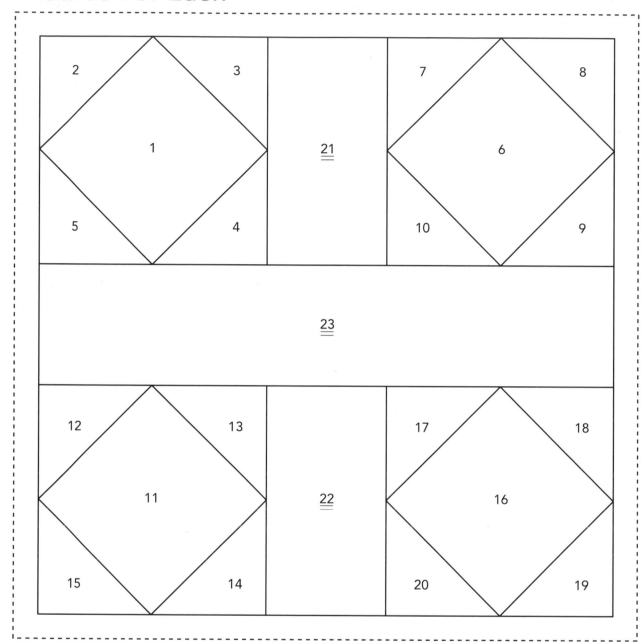

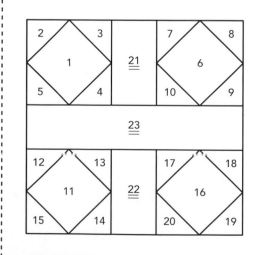

Garden of Eden

14 Combo: Partial Piecing, Seams Colliding, and Flip-Flopping
(Triple Link Chain and Indian Meadows)

INTRODUCTION

If you have worked your way from the beginning of the book, you now know all the basic principles of Flip-Flop Paper Piecing. All flip-flop foundation blocks—and there are thousands—can be sewn using one or more of these principles in sometimes obvious, and sometimes not so obvious, ways.

Most of the blocks in the previous chapters were fairly simple. But do not be deceived. Although basic blocks may be best for instructional purposes, Flip-Flop Paper Piecing can apply to, and simplify the construction of, many a complex geometric block.

At its most glorious, Flip-Flop Paper Piecing can help you construct a complicated block composed of multiple pieces using multiple techniques. The result is a how-did-you-do-that moment when the single foundation on the flip side of the block is flashed into sight. I love that moment. I live for that moment.

Triple Link Chain is constructed entirely on a single piece of paper. What is new with this block is that it uses a combination of multiple techniques—in this case Ring Around the Circle with Partial Seam Piecing (Chapter 6), When Seams Collide (Chapter 4), and The Basic Flip-Flop (Chapter 2).

WARNING

Do *not* look at the entire Highlighted Instructional Block for Triple Link Chain all at once. It can be scary. It scares me, and I just made it. I promise you, it is *far* easier than it looks. Just tackle one simple numbered piece at a time. Bit by bit, you'll move along. Before you know it, the whole, dandy block will be done. Remember, you've already learned every single maneuver needed to complete the entire block, start to finish.

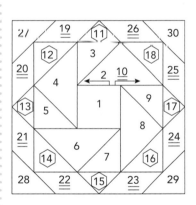

Foundation with Instructions

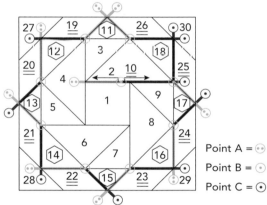

Highlighted Instructional Block

Point A = ⊗
Point B = ⊙
Point C = ⊙

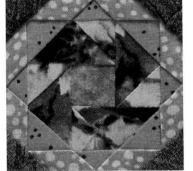

Completed Block: Triple Link Chain

TRIPLE LINK CHAIN BLOCK CONSTRUCTION

Unless otherwise specified, your stitched seamline should be ¼" longer than the printed line at each side, extending into an adjacent piece at each end.

1. Place piece 1 right side up on the unprinted Fabric Side. Place piece 2/10 right side down on top of piece 1.

2. Sew the first leg, starting at Point A and stopping at Point B. This is the partial seam.

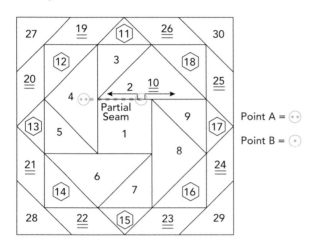

Point A = ⊙⊙
Point B = ⊙

Sew partial seam.

3. Insert pins at Points B and C to mark the seamline for the second leg. Go straight up from the Printed Side through to the unprinted Fabric Side. Place a ruler over piece 2/10 from Point B through Point C. Draw a chalk line to mark the seamline for the second leg. Remove the pins.

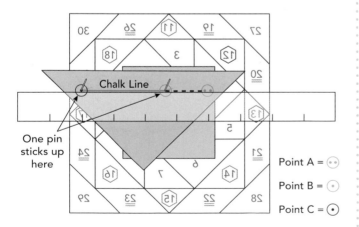

Point A = ⊙⊙
Point B = ⊙
Point C = ⊙

Draw chalk line to mark unsewn seamline of piece 2/10.

4. Fold along the marked line and press into place. The folded seamline is the unsewn portion of the partial seam. It will be sewn (or fused) later. Do **not** sew the folded portion of the seam at this time.

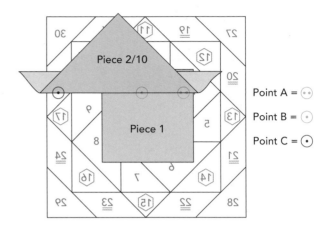

Point A = ⊙⊙
Point B = ⊙
Point C = ⊙

Press. Do *not* sew between Points B and C.

5. Sew pieces 3–7 as you would in traditional foundation piecing (pages 9–10).

6. Pin piece 2/10 out of the way. Then sew pieces 8 and 9 as you would in traditional foundation piecing.

7. Unpin piece 2/10 and press it back into place. Sew or fuse the second leg from the unprinted Fabric Side (pages 17–18).

8. Sew piece 11 from Point B to Point B, dot to dot precisely, then press it into place.

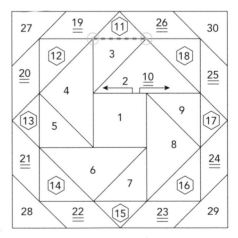

Point B = ⊙

Sew piece 11 from Point B to Point B precisely.

9. Sew pieces 12–18 exactly as you sewed piece 11 (Step 8).

10. Sew the first leg of flip-flop piece 19 from the Printed Side, first pinning the protruding seam allowance of piece 12 out of the way. Remove the pin and press the seam allowance of piece 12 back into place.

11. Sew or fuse the second leg of piece 19 from the unprinted Fabric Side (pages 17–18).

12. Sew flip-flop pieces 20–26 exactly as you sewed piece 19 (Steps 10–11).

13. Sew pieces 27–30 as you would in traditional foundation piecing.

PRACTICE YOUR SKILLS: INDIAN MEADOWS

Indian Meadows is a beautiful combination block. Although it looks hard, it is not. It's all done with basic flip-flops (not even Seams Colliding) and a single From Outside In maneuver. Review The Basic Flip-Flop (pages 14–19) and From Outside In (pages 69–70) if you need a refresher; otherwise, you're good to go.

Refrain from looking at the scary Highlighted Instructional Block all at once. Just follow the block construction number-by-number, checking the Highlighted Instructional Block only if you have any doubt about which leg goes first. As a matter of fact, because the surface is smooth for each flip-flop piece (3, 5, 7, 10, 12, 14, and 16), either leg *could* go first. I prefer the added strength of the sewn seams to be those radiating toward the center of each flower. For that reason only, I suggest my green versus red leg selection.

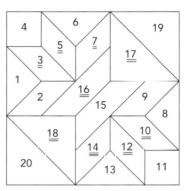

Foundation with Instructions   Highlighted Instructional Block

Point A = ⊙⊙
Point B = ⊙
Point C = ⊙

Completed Block: Indian Meadows

Triple Link Chain

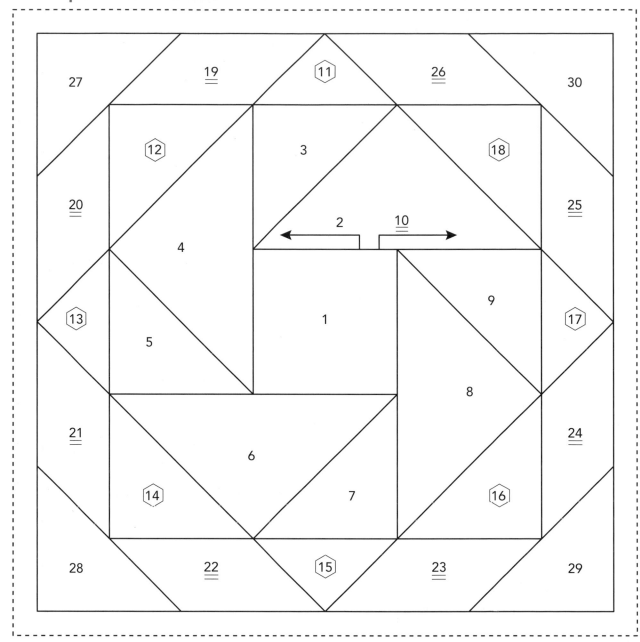

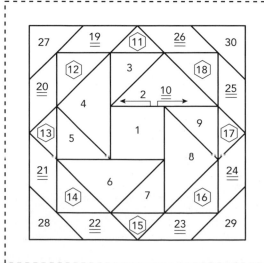

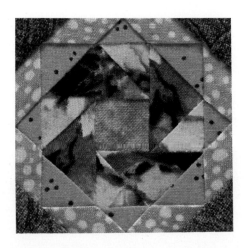

Indian Meadows

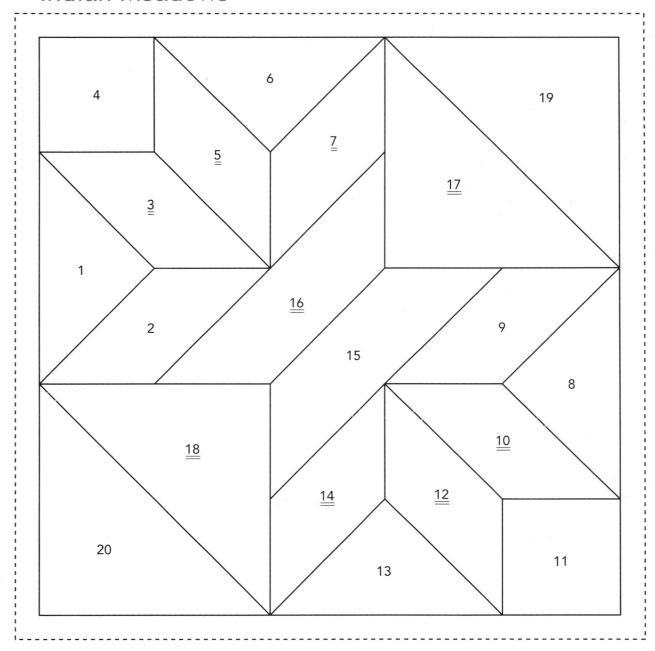

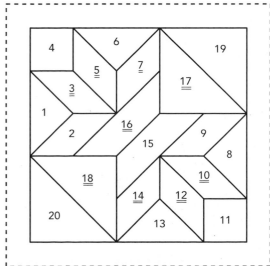

15 Flip-Flop Sampler

Choose your favorite 25 blocks from the preceding chapters and put them together into one fantastic *Flip-Flop Sampler*. My version is wallhanging or lap-sized. However, this quilt could be made bed-sized by adding more blocks and/or wider borders. To maintain the scrappy sampler look, simply make any duplicate blocks from a different selection of fabric. My pictured sampler contains a repeat of Jewel (Chapter 3).

Finished blocks: 6″ × 6″. Finished quilt: 36½″ × 56½″

MATERIALS

3¼ yards total of assorted prints for blocks and appliqué

½ yard dark, subtle tone-on-tone fabric for sashing strips and squares

1¼ yards light, subtle tone-on-tone fabric for sashing strips, squares, and appliqué background

1¾ yards for backing

½ yard for binding

Batting: 40″ × 60″

Steam-A-Seam 2: ¼″-wide roll (Regular, not Lite)

CUTTING

Dark Fabric

Cut 60 rectangles 1″ × 6½″.

Cut 72 squares 1″ × 1″.

Light Fabric

Cut 60 rectangles 1″ × 6½″.

Cut 72 squares 1″ × 1″.

Cut 2 rectangles 37½″ × 11½″ for appliqué background. (Appliqué, then trim to 36½″ × 10½″.)

Binding Fabric

Cut 5 strips 2¼″ × width of the fabric.

BLOCK ASSEMBLY

Make 25 blocks. Do not remove the foundation paper yet.

SASHING ASSEMBLY AND QUILT CONSTRUCTION

Because each block was constructed flip-flop style on a 6″ piece of paper, each block will finish at exactly 6″. This accuracy makes pieced sashing construction a dream come true. Press all seams open to produce flatter seams and a smoother area for quilting.

1. Sew a light sashing strip to a dark sashing strip. Make 60. Press.

Make 60.

2. Sew a light sashing square to a dark sashing square. Make 72. Press.

Make 72.

3. Piece together 2 units. Make 36. Press.

Make 36.

4. Sew the sashing and blocks into rows, as shown in the Assembly Diagram. Sew the rows together. Press.

 NOTE: The dark and light fabrics alternate from row to row.

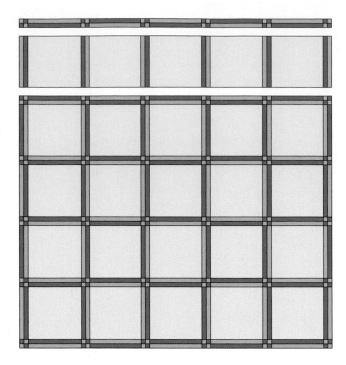

Assembly Diagram

5. Enlarge the appliqué pattern (pages 85–86) to 125%.

6. Prepare and stitch the appliqué pieces to the background rectangles using your preferred method. Use embroidery for the stems and tendrils and beads for the small circular motifs.

NOTE: Because the appliqué design is a mirror image, the pattern should be used right side up for the top border and upside down for the bottom border.

7. Trim and sew the appliqué border sections to the pieced section of the quilt top.

8. Spray starch everything firmly in place, then remove the paper from the pieced blocks.

9. Layer the quilt top, batting, and backing. Quilt and then bind.

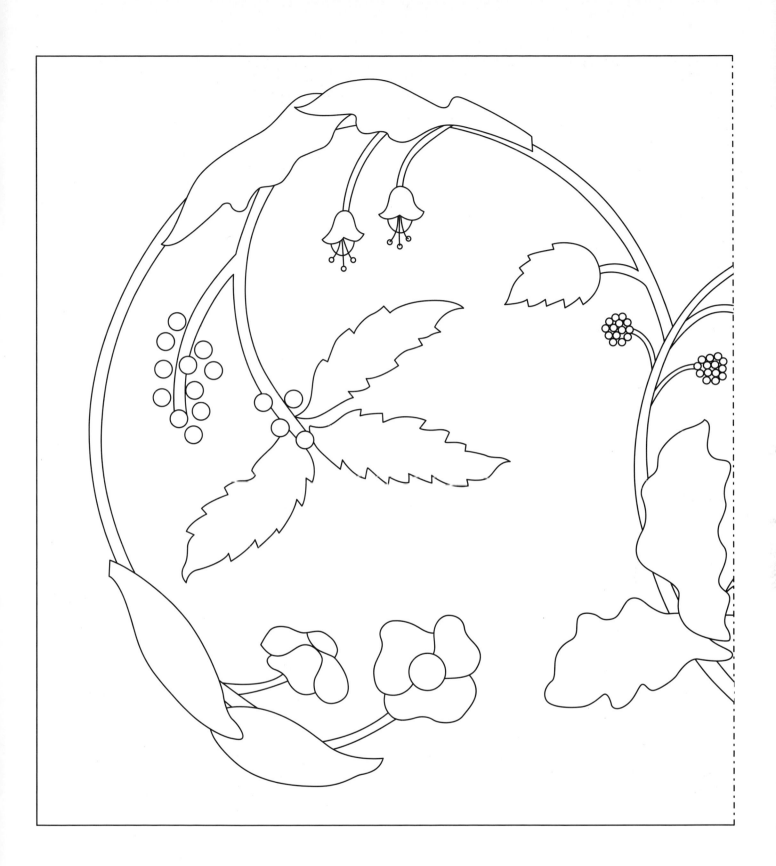

Fold

16 Quilt Gallery

Original artwork by Edna Eicke, courtesy of *The New Yorker*.

New York Beauty, 52″ × 66″, by Mary Kay Mouton

This quilt started it all! I had a collection of Halloween prints and was determined to use them in a pieced border. I had reason to suspect that my pieced blocks would not be the size they were supposed to be. They never were. With that knowledge in mind, I scattered New York Beauty blocks along the border, providing myself with a fudge factor: Those blocks could be enlarged or contracted as needed to make the final border the right size.

In addition to producing a frame for my appliqué, my goal in terms of the pieced border was to audition every available piecing technique to find the best one for achieving uniform results and sharp, precise geometric shapes.

I tried one technique after another, with varying degrees of success, until I fumbled into Flip-Flop Paper Piecing while trying to match a plaid without fussy cutting individual pieces. Once I performed that first basic flip-flop maneuver, my mind was flooded with one variation after another.

I have since made several quilts that have been pieced flip-flop style, but *New York Beauty* will always be my favorite.

New Technique, Desperately Need Publisher, 17″ × 21½″, by Mary Kay Mouton

This was the second quilt I made using Flip-Flop Paper Piecing. It was small scale, made with the confident intent of fully exploring the new technique.

I just stopped at forty-one 3″ blocks, and then successfully submitted the quilt to the judges at the yearly American Quilter's Society competition. They told me that 3″ was too large for a miniature block. However, they also said they were pleased with the precision with which the points all met. I've since done 2¼″ and then 1½″ blocks. There is, indeed, nothing like foundation piecing for painless precision. And with Flip-Flop Paper Piecing, a single, undivided foundation can be used to produce thousands of blocks—a range large enough to satisfy the Dear Jane-iest piecer among us.

Simply Delectable, 44¾″ × 44¾″,
by Mary Kay Mouton

As a lifelong fan of Delectable
Mountain, I couldn't help trying
my hand at a mix of the 6″ version
in the main body of the quilt, with
the 2¼″ miniature in the border.
(See page 39 for piecing directions.)
One simple flip-flopped piece is all
I needed to turn this block into a
foundation-pieced quickie.

Pastel Flip-Flop Sampler,
30″ × 41¼″, by Mary Kay Mouton

This project was made to try out a
soft, springtime palette instead of
my usual fall colors.

King's X's and Big O's, 25″ × 33″, by Mary Kay Mouton

This quilt was made using only two blocks, both set on point: King's X from Chapter 7 and Big O from Chapter 6. It certainly turned out to be a very masculine-looking little number when the turquoise I had planned for the Big O's looked simply horrible with my King's X background. Quilts do sometimes dictate their own destiny.

Delectable Christmas, 26″ × 26″, by Angeline Mouton

This quilt, which includes Delectable Mountain and a sampler border, was made by my daughter during her Christmas vacation. All blocks are either featured in the preceding chapters or constructed using techniques presented in this book. She proved to me that it is possible to flip-flop your way through 20 blocks in a day. She is faster than I'll ever be.

Christmas Star Pillow, 13½″ × 13½″, by Kathy Boylan

This pillow features a LeMoyne Star, a traditional block that can be flip-flop pieced using techniques learned in Chapter 4, "When Seams Collide," and Chapter 7, "Two Become One." The assembly sequence is that used in Indian Meadows (page 79).

Springtime Stars, 9″ × 23¾″, by Betty Ivey

This table runner comprises three LeMoyne Stars flip-flop pieced with the techniques presented in Chapters 4 and 7. The assembly sequence is the one explained in Indian Meadows (page 79).

An assortment of blocks from Chapters 2–5, each finished
6″ × 6″, all by Elizabeth Scott

This is a complete collection of all the blocks featured in
Chapters 2–5. I see a sampler in the making.

Appendix
Green Leg Versus Red Leg

Determining which of the legs of a flip-flop piece to sew first (the green leg versus red leg) is not random. There is a method that determines the best choice. The decision made will affect the quality of the block, as well as the ease with which its seams are sewn.

SECOND (RED) LEG NEEDS A SMOOTH SURFACE

The reasoning behind the selection is that the second leg (red leg), which will be sewn or fused from the Fabric Side, must have a perfectly smooth surface for application. As you sew or fuse this second leg, you do not want a seam allowance from a previously sewn seam to be in your way. Rather, you want a lovely, flat surface for that red leg.

FIRST LEG CONFRONTS SEAM ALLOWANCE

Because the second leg cannot have a seam allowance in its way, if there is a seam allowance, then it must be a part of the construction of the first leg. When you are sewing that first leg, it is quite easy to pin any pesky seam allowance out of the way before you sew from the Printed Side. In addition, the tight stitching you make as you machine sew the first leg will ensure that a projecting, annoying seam allowance will stay out of the way as you complete the second leg.

SELECTING WHICH SEAM IS WHICH

There are two approaches to guarantee that the right choice is made when facing a green leg versus red leg selection.

1. By Sight

Look at the Printed Side of both legs to be sewn. Then flip the foundation and look at the same legs from the unprinted Fabric Side. (See illustration.) Does one of the legs have a seam poking into it? If so, that leg is the first leg (green leg). Which leg is smooth from the outside edge all the way down to the tip? That is the second leg (red leg). If neither leg has a seam poking into it, then it doesn't matter which leg is sewn first.

2. By Touch

Find the two legs in question on the Printed Side, then flip to the unprinted Fabric Side. On the Fabric Side, run your finger along both legs to be sewn. Start at the outside edge (generally at Point A or Point C) and run your finger along the seamline toward Point B. If you run into a seam allowance before you hit Point B, then that is the first leg (green leg). If you don't run into a seam allowance and it's a smooth run from the outside edge (Point A or Point C) all the way to Point B, then that is the second leg (red leg). If neither seam allowance has a seam poking into it, then it doesn't matter which leg is sewn first.

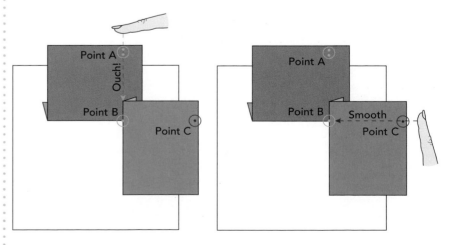

First leg (green): run into a seam allowance

Second Leg (red): smooth all the way to Point B

Resources

Steam-A-Seam 2, ¼" rolls (Regular, not Lite) can be obtained from:

CLOTILDE

P.O. Box 7500

Big Sandy, TX 75755

(800) 772-2891

www.clotilde.com

THE WARM COMPANY

(800) 234-WARM (9276)

www.warmcompany.com (will direct you to a nearby retail store)

For a list of other fine books from C&T Publishing, ask for a free catalog:

C&T PUBLISHING, INC.

P.O. Box 1456

Lafayette, CA 94549

(800) 284-1114

Email: ctinfo@ctpub.com

www.ctpub.com

C&T Publishing's professional photography services are now available to the public. Visit us at www.ctmediaservices.com.

For quilting supplies:

COTTON PATCH

1025 Brown Avenue

Lafayette, CA 94549

Store: (925) 284-1177

Mail order: (925) 283-7883

Email: CottonPa@aol.com

www.quiltusa.com

Note: Fabrics used in the quilts shown may not be currently available, as fabric manufacturers keep most fabrics in print for only a short time.

About the Author

Mary Kay Mouton is an award-winning quiltmaker whose works have been juried into numerous national competitions. Her first quilt was a foundation-pieced Log Cabin made in the late 1970s. Since that time, she has experimented with a full range of piecing techniques. More recently, she returned to foundation piecing with a vow never more to wander. She paraphrases Scarlett O'Hara and promises that as heaven is her witness, she will never piece without paper again.

Great Titles
from  C&T PUBLISHING

 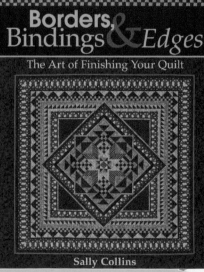 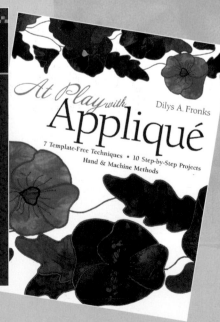